When the Lord Made the Tempter

By Donald Peart

Edition: September 2022

ISBN: 978-0-9886897-0

Table of Contents

Acknowledgments

I honor our Lord Jesus Christ, my Savior, who has been given "all authority ... in heaven and on earth." I give honor to the Spirit of Jesus who have been my teacher from the beginning. I also honor the men and women of God who have taught me through the years.

Comment

It seems appropriate to comment on the purpose of this book. I would like to say on the onset that this book is written to show that the tempter, called the serpent, is junior to mankind. That is, the tempter cannot usurp authority over us because the Lord created mankind before the tempter. This "tempter" is also known as the serpent that deceived Mrs. Adam. Yet above all the seniority the Lord has given us is the seniority through the Lord Jesus Christ that he possesses over all creation.

That is, Jesus holds absolute superpower and super-authority over all creation, including but not limited to, the tempter. This book is also written to highlight Biblical principles that refute many of the erroneous teachings relative to the tempter. There are many doctrines being taught that are out of line with God's point of view; and I do understand that some of these teachings were passed down from past generations, and thus difficult to let go.

With that said, I also recommend that the reader read one of my other books, titled, *Exousia, Your God Given Authority.* In *Exousia, Your God Given Authority,* I show in detail the "authority" Jesus has given us (His saints) over all the "power"[1] of the enemy; and the book also reveals the defeated state the tempter now lives in, through the conquest of Jesus. I also provided some documentation of signs, miracles and wonders the Lord Jesus performed through my wife and I which indeed show the authority of His Christ in the lives of believers.

---

[1] "Power" cannot work without "authority." In the book of Acts, the snake that bit Paul had the "power" to bite Paul; however, the snake's bite or venom had no "authority" over Paul to harm Paul. Paul shook off the serpent and continued with what he was doing with no affect to Paul's body from the serpent's bite.

Introduction

On a day during the early 1990s, I was really disheartened and speaking to the Lord about my situation. At the time, we were experiencing extreme trails as I was being obedient to instructions the Lord had given me. I was to give myself to study of His Word for what turned out to be about four years of intense study and prayer coupled with what I define as also a time of consistent acute trials.

As I sat on the sofa that day reading Genesis 2, I began to understand what I was reading in Genesis in a way I was not taught by my elders. The Spirit of the Lord began to show me the sequence of creation, including the man (Adam), the serpent, and Mrs. Adam, (later called Eve).

As the Spirit of Jesus was revealing to me "how" the Scriptures in Genesis 2 are really read, my mind began to question what I was reading in the Spirit. As I continues to question what the Holy Spirit was revealing to me, I was reminded of an encounter Jesus had with a lawyer who had some questions about the Scriptures and the manner in which Jesus responded to the lawyer relative to the lawyer's question?

Jesus enlightened the lawyer by indicating that the Scriptures are only understood properly based on "how" they are read (Luke 10:26).

Luke 10:25-26: *25And, behold, a certain lawyer stood up, and tempted him, saying, Master, what shall I do to inherit eternal life? 26He said unto him, what is written in the law?* **How read you?**

This same lesson on "how" to read the Scriptures was in direct conflict with what I thought the Scripture meant as the Lord was opening to me Genesis 2. At that moment in the vision, I was receiving a lesson from the Spirit of Jesus on "how" to read the Scriptures; yet my mind questioned the revelation of the Holy Spirit due to previous doctrines I learned in Church from elders and commentaries.

As I questioned what I understood from God, because of what I was previously taught; in the Spirit, I saw the pages of the Bible I was reading closed one by one, yet the physical Bible in my lap was still open to the same pages I was reading.[2] (This is when I realized I was seeing a vision.) The Lord then said to me, *"Do not filter my Word through what you were taught by the elders."* He then instructed me to go and study the Scripture to see "how" the Scriptures should be read and understood based on what He had just showed me in Genesis 2 relative to creation. I was to study, especially, when did the Lord actually make the tempter, called the serpent? This book is a result of that research.

Some of the preachers (including commentaries written by preachers) who were teaching me "errors" (maybe inadvertently) apparently fulfilled the words of Isaiah 9:14-16: "Therefore the LORD will cut off **head** and tail from Israel, palm branch and bulrush in one day. The **elder** and honorable, he is the **head**; the prophet who teaches lies, he is the tail. **For the leaders of this people cause them to err,** and those who are led by them are destroyed."

Imagine what our Lord faced when He came on the scene and began to change **"old time"** doctrines. Here is an example of Jesus challenging the "old time" doctrines. "You have heard that it was said by them of **old time,** you shall not commit adultery; **but I say unto you** that whoever looks at a woman to lust after her has committed adultery with he already in his heart" (See Matthew 5:21; 5:27; 5:33). With, that said, we are not to ignore all the teaching of the elders. The Bible teaches that some traditions are to be held (2 Thessalonians 2:15).

The Bible is only a closed book if we try to filter God's writings through the doctrines of men. In the words of Dr. Kelley Varner, "there is only one thing more powerful than the Word of God, the traditions of men that make "the Word of God of non-effect."[3] Dr. Varner concluded this from what our Lord Jesus taught. Jesus

---

[2] The cover of this book was designed based on this vision.
[3] Please refer to Mark 7:3-13; Matthew 15:2-3

taught, that the Pharisees and Scribes made "the word of God of **none effect** through [their] **tradition** ..." (Mark 7:13). Thus, I learned to read the Bible slowly to make sure I read what it says, and not what I was taught by some elders that it supposedly said.

We are not to attempt to make the Bible fit our understanding; we are to conform our understanding to God's exegete. I teach that we should not **bend** the Bible to fit our lifestyle; if we are not living what the Bible said. On the contrary, we teach the Bible as it says even though we may not be living what it says. The Pharisees, contrary to God's Word, changed the commands of God to fit their traditions. Let us teach what the Bible says, as the Lord has also commanded me, saying, "Son of man, speak to the house of Israel with **my words.**" We are to teach the saints with **"His words;"** not bending His Word with our words to make them fit our traditions. Therefore, as you read this book, verify this teaching by the Bible (Acts 17:10-11).

Jesus' Blood Speaks

Hebrews 12:22; 24, NKJ: *22But you have come …. 24to Jesus …the blood of sprinkling that speaks better things than that of Abel.*

Revelation 12:11, NKJ: *And they overcame him by the blood of the Lamb ….*

Colossians 3:18, NKJ: *And He is the head of the body, the church, who is the beginning, the firstborn from the dead, that in all things He may have the preeminence.*

Jesus has the preeminence over all creation. Thus, I will speak of the Lord's blood that was shed for us and the "strength" of His blood that overcomes all, including but not limited to, the great dragon. Jesus, the Christ, offered His blood for our salvation; and "we preach not ourselves, but Christ Jesus the Lord" (1 Corinthians 4:5). It is important that I begin this book by preaching Jesus and the power of His blood that was shed for us. It is also appropriate that I will also conclude this book with the blood of Jesus that is a boundary against all principalities, authorities, dominions, "world-strengths," powers, etcetera. May Jesus' blood, be upon all the words of this book in order to bring about an overcoming life by believing that Jesus is the Christ and the strength of Jesus' blood.

The Lamb of God — Jesus, the Christ — offered His blood for us. This was of utmost importance because "without shedding of blood there is no **remission**" of sins and/or guilt (see Hebrews 9:22). God purchased us with the "price of blood" — **the Lamb's** (1 Corinthians 6:20; 1 Corinthians 7:23; Matthew 27:6; Acts 20:28). The Lamb's blood that was offered for us is a key, because without the blood of Jesus we cannot rid ourselves of any guilt in order to approach God.

Things pertaining to bloodguilt — blood of abortion, blood of murder, blood of adultery, blood of incest, blood of not honoring parents, blood of homosexuality, bloodshed from violence, blood of wars, and even bloodguilt of not preaching the gospel of Jesus are one of the most critical things among humanity. Bloodshed is such a serious item with the Lord that He judged even the animals for shedding man's blood (Exodus 9:5-6). However, there is relief for the nations from the guilt of bloodshed.

The blood of the Lamb is that blood that overcomes the **"voice"** of every bloodguilt that sometimes prevents humanity from approaching God. We can only be released to approach God by the strongest blood covenant that was ever ratified. God wants us to hear His voice (the voice of Jesus' blood) as we approach Him. He does not want us to be hearing the **voices** of any other blood. You may wonder how this is possible. It is possible because the blood of the Lamb **"speaks** better things" in our conscience. The voice of the blood of Jesus is **"stronger"** than the voice of any other blood. Yes, Jesus' blood has a voice!

Hebrews 12:22-24, NKJ: *22But you have come …. 24to Jesus the Mediator of the new covenant, and to the **blood** of sprinkling that **speaks better** things than that of Abel.*

Genesis 4:8-10, NKJ: *8Now Cain talked with Abel his brother; and it came to pass, when they were in the field, that Cain rose up against Abel his brother and killed him. 9Then the LORD said to Cain, "Where is Abel your brother?" He said, "I do not know. Am I my brother's keeper?" 10And He said, "What have you done? The **voice** of your brother's **blood cries out** to Me from the ground.*

Jesus came to deliver mankind from the **"voice"** of bloodguilt. There are many in the world tormented by the voice of blood that they have shed on the earth. Some are not even aware of the things that are associated with blood which cause guilt. However, God has remedied that effect of bloodguilt through the voice of a **"better"** blood. Allow me to explain. I presume that you have heard of the many adverse effects that abortion has on the parents, particularly the mother of the fetus that was terminated. The guilt that is felt by the parents of the fetus, after an abortion is committed, is really the **"voice"** of the baby's blood.

In Genesis 4:8-10, stated above, Cain killed his brother Abel. The Lord then stated that Abel's **"blood [the victim's] cries out."** The same text also stated that blood has a "**voice**" — "the **voice** of your brother's blood cries out to [God]." This is true for any bloodshed — murder, adultery, abortion, hating parents, etc.

The blood of the aborted babies or the blood of any victim has a voice. We call it guilt. The replay of the feeling of guilt is the voice of the victim's blood crying out for vengeance. The good news is: The blood of the Lamb can overpower the voice of any blood that was shed. (Note: This does not mean that a person is exempt from the legal system if blood is shed against the law. You can be forgiven by God, and still get disciplined by the laws of the land for shedding blood.)

Jesus' "**blood** … **speaks better** things than … Abel." If there is an "Abel" in your history the voice of the blood of Jesus is stronger than the guilt of your conscience. "Better" is the Greek word "**kreítton**" which literally means "**stronger**," "**to hold**." The root for this word is "**kratos**" which is transliterated as "**great**" in our English language.

The blood of the Lamb is "**greater**" than any bloodguilt we may have. The **voice** of Jesus' blood is "**stronger**" in our conscience than any other voices. In fact, His blood only allows one voice to rule in our heart. That is to say, His blood "**holds**" us to voice of His forgiveness. His blood takes away the consciousness of evil.

One of the reasons why many will not consider serving God is the conscience "accusing" a person with guilt that has been imprinted on their conscience. Some of the bloodguilt on the conscience is not even obvious. However, the guilt is still there. Before I discuss our conscience becoming purged by the Blood of Jesus; let us look at a list of items that generate bloodguilt.

*Leviticus 20:9, NKJ: For everyone who **curses (lit., make light)** his father or his mother shall surely be put to death. He has **cursed** his father or his mother. **His blood shall be upon him.***

Those who curse his/her father or mother are guilty of blood. In Mark 7:10 "curse" is two Greek words used together, "kakos" (evil or bad) and "logos" (word). This is strong, in light of this generation. We cannot take our parents "lightly" or speak "bad words," regardless of the sins of our parents.

*Leviticus 20:11, NKJ: **The man who lays with his father's wife** has uncovered his father's nakedness; both of them shall surely be put to death. **Their blood shall be upon them.***

This happened in the New Testament (1 Corinthians 5:1). The guilty person was originally slated by Paul for death by Satan (1 Corinthians 5:5). The verdict of death was passed by a foundation ministry — an apostle. The point: Sexual immorality is like shedding blood which causes guilt.

*Leviticus 20:12, NKJ: If a man lies with his daughter-in-law, both of them shall surely be put to death. They have committed perversion. **Their blood shall be upon them.***

My wife and I walked a young lady out of a situation like this. Incest can be damaging to both parties. The daughter-in-law and the "man" who initiated the sexual perversion become guilty of blood, especially, if the daughter-in-law is a virgin. **"Their"** blood is upon **"them."** The blood guilt of her broken virginity (the hymen) now affects the abused also, hence the plural "their" and "them." Sexual sins are related to blood.

*Leviticus 20:13, NKJ: **If a man lies with a male as he lies with a woman**, both of them have committed an abomination. They shall surely be put to death. **Their blood shall be upon them.***

Blood is also shed during homoerotic acts. The word for covenant according to the Holy Writ means to cut flesh in two pieces where blood flow and then pass between the fleshes. When a man's penis passes through the flesh (hind parts) of another man, an unclean covenant is initiated, and blood covenant is involved through friction. **"Their blood** shall be upon them" — both.

Leviticus 20:15-16, NKJ: [15]*If a man mates with an animal, he shall surely be put to death, and you shall kill the animal.* [16]*If a **woman approaches any animal and mates with it**, you shall kill the woman* and the animal. They shall surely be put to death. **Their blood is upon them.**

Bestiality is a crime punishable by death according to God. There is blood guilt involved. For the Church goers, the woman (the apostate Church) who approaches the beast system (Revelation 17:3) is guilty of the blood of Jesus. Man, or woman should not sleep with beast/animals naturally or spiritually.

*Ezekiel 16:38, NKJ: And I will judge you as women who **break wedlock** or shed blood are judged; I will bring blood upon you in fury and jealousy.*

Breaking wedlock is the same **as** shedding blood. In the word of the prophet Ezekiel, breaking wedlock and shedding blood are equated. Blood will be **brought** upon adulterers by the Lord. Let me say it another way; when a marriage is consummated a blood, covenant is established at "marriage sex," even if the couples are not virgins.

Yes, the virgin's hymen in the woman is there for covenant. In addition, every time a man and a woman come together blood is involved. The blood may be in the "micro" dimension, but it is still present. Also, remember the definition I gave earlier for covenant. Thus, blood guilt is involved in adultery, and it should be resolved through the stronger blood of Jesus.

One can see from the many Scriptures cited in this section, blood guilt ranges from disrespect towards parents to sleeping with an animal. It follows that the conscience of humanity is in a tailspin through the guilt of blood. There are many voices inside the head of humanity crying, "Guilty, guilty." This is one of the reasons why the blood of Jesus is so important to our conscience. We cannot serve God without our conscience being purged and made good by the blood of Christ.

Hebrews 9:13-14, NKJ: [13]*For if the blood of bulls and goats and the ashes of a heifer, sprinkling the unclean, sanctifies for the purifying of the flesh,* [14]*how much more shall the **blood of Christ**, who through the **eternal***

*Spirit offered Himself without spot to God, **cleanse your conscience** from dead works to serve the living God?*

***Hebrews 10:22, NKJ:** Let us draw near with a true heart in full assurance of faith, having our **hearts sprinkled from an evil conscience** and our bodies washed with pure water.*

Revelation 7:14, NKJ:** ... These are the ones who ... washed their robes and made them white in the **blood of the Lamb.

The conscience is that voice of guilt that speaks to people when they are alone on their beds at night, thinking on the guilt of their lives. It is this consciousness that Jesus' blood can quiet with the sweet voice of His blood that was shed for you and me. Aren't you tired of always feeling bad from guilt—the guilt the Bible calls an "evil conscience," or a "consciousness of evil?" We can have a "better" conscience through the blood of Jesus. "Conscience" means "co-perception," or to have two perceptions.

There are two perceptions of evil. A person may believe that he/she is so evil that forgiveness cannot be realized, and at the same time, want to believe that God has indeed forgiven him/her. The consciousness of evil is to believe the former. The consciousness of good is to believe the latter—the blood of Jesus, through the eternal Spirit does indeed deliver from the guilt of sin. The question is how does a person realize the better blood of Jesus? How do we become conscious of good <u>in lieu</u> of consciousness of evil? Let me begin answering these questions with a question. Have you ever seen the blood of Jesus that was shed 2000 years ago? The answer is no! Yet, we (the Believers in Jesus) claim that the blood of Jesus works today, and it does work today. Therefore, the blood is also **spiritual**. Let me explain.

***Hebrews 9:14, NKJ:** How much more shall the **blood of Christ**, who through the **eternal Spirit** offered Himself without spot to God, **cleanse your conscience** from dead works to serve the living God?*

John 6:53-56; 63, NKJ: *[54]**Whoever eats My flesh and drinks My blood has eternal life,** and I will raise him up at the last day. [55]For My flesh is food indeed, and My blood is drink indeed. [56]He who eats My flesh* *and drinks My blood abides in Me, and I in him .... ⁶³It is the Spirit who gives life; the flesh profits nothing.* **The words that I speak to you are spirit, and they are life.**

Jesus, before He died, I repeat, before He died, told some of His followers that they had to drink His blood. They thought He was crazy and stopped following Him (John 6:60 w/John 6:66). However, Jesus knew exactly what He was talking about, and gave the explanation. **"It is the Spirit who gives life;** the flesh profits nothing. **The words that I speak to you are spirit, and they are life."**

Before Jesus died and rose again, He linked the Holy Spirit to His blood and body. They could drink His blood through the Holy Spirit. The blood of Jesus is related to the Spirit of the Lord. Hebrews 9:14, quoted above, states that the blood of Jesus is linked to the **"eternal Spirit."** This is one of the reasons why Jesus' blood is as potent in the conscience today as it was on the day He was crucified. In fact, He was slain before the world was created. Therefore, the followers in John, Chapter 6, could appropriate the blood of the Lamb through the Holy Spirit.

1 Peter 1:19-20, NKJ: *¹⁹but with* **the precious blood of Christ, as of a lamb** *without blemish and without spot.* *²⁰***He indeed was foreordained before the foundation of the world but** *was manifest in these last times for you.*

Revelation 13:8, NKJ: *All who dwell on the earth will worship him, whose names have not been written in the Book of Life of* **the Lamb slain from the foundation** *of the world.*

The same is true today. The blood of Jesus can be applied to the conscience through the eternal Spirit. In other words, the sacrifice of Jesus is as fresh as it was approximately two thousand years ago. His blood that was shed for us is always **"new"** and His blood is full of life. His blood is **"living,"** and His blood applied to our conscience causes us to "serve the **living** God."

Hebrews 10:19-20, NKJ: [19] *Therefore, brethren, having boldness to enter the Holiest by the blood of Jesus,* [20] *by a **new** and living way which He consecrated for us, through the veil, that is, His flesh.*

According to <u>Vines Expository Dictionary</u>, the word **"new"** in verse 20 above **(Greek, prosphatos),** originally signified **"freshly slain."** Jesus is the **"recently"** slain sacrifice for every age. In reality, He was only slain the day before yesterday. One day with the Lord is as a thousand (2 Peter 3:8). Two thousand years ago is the day before yesterday to God. In addition, He is freshly (recently) slain because one of His omnipresent manifestations is **"as"** a slain Lamb.

*Revelation 5:6, NKJ: And I looked, and behold, in the midst of the throne and of the four living creatures, and in the midst of the elders, stood a Lamb **as though** it had been slain…*

*Revelation 5:6, NASU: And I saw between the throne (with the four living creatures) and the elders a Lamb standing, **as if** slain…*

The Scripture is the authority. It cannot be denied. This is one of the Lamb's omnipresent manifestations. Proof: The Lamb was in more than one place at the same time, in the verse stated above. He was "in the midst of the throne." At the same time, He was in the "midst … of the four living creatures." In addition, He was also "in the midst …of the elders." The Lamb was omnipresent in the middle of all the entities listed above, plus more.

The omnipresent Lamb is on His throne (Revelation 3:21). He is in us—His Church (Colossians 1:27). "The Lord is the Spirit" (2 Corinthians 3:17), etc. The Lord is everywhere being all who He is to everyone—He is omnipresent. It follows that one of His omnipresent manifestations is that of **"Lamb … as if slain."** Thus, His blood and sacrifice are as fresh today as it was the day before yesterday. This truth is made experiential through the eternal Spirit. The blood of the Lamb is linked to the Spirit of the Lord. As it is written: "…the **blood of Christ**, who through the **eternal Spirit** offered Himself without spot to God, **cleanses your conscience** from dead works to serve the living God" (Hebrews 9:14)?

The blood of the Lamb speaks in such a way that our conscience can be conscious of the good words of the blood of Jesus, as opposed to the bad words of the blood of guilt. The blood of the Lamb reconciled us to hear the good words out of heaven again, in this life. The blood of Jesus also reconciled things on heaven.

Colossians 1:19-20, NKJ: *19For it pleased the Father that in Him all the fullness should dwell, 20and by Him to **reconcile all things** to Himself, by Him, whether things on earth or **things in heaven,** having made **peace through the blood** of His cross.*

Soon after the Lord's blood brought me into fellowship with Him again, I read this verse. After reading it, I questioned why the blood of Jesus had to reconcile "things in heaven." It did not make sense to me because Adam sinned on the earth, so I thought. Adam did sin on the earth. However, that is not completely true. The fact is Adam sinned in heaven. Thus, the heavens had to be reconciled. Let me explain!

2 Corinthians 12:2-4, NKJ: *2I know a man in Christ who fourteen years ago--whether in the body I do not know, or whether out of the body I do not know, God knows--such a one was caught up to **the third heaven.** 3And I know such a man--whether in the body or out of the body I do not know, God knows — 4how he was caught up into **Paradise** ...*

Paul called "the third heaven" "Paradise." This is pretty straightforward. The next question is, "What is Paradise?" According to Jesus, through the apostle John whom the Lord loves, Paradise is the place where the tree of life exists.

Revelation 2:7, NKJ: *He who has an ear, let him hear what the Spirit says to the churches. To him who overcomes I will give to eat from **the tree of life,** which is in the **midst** of the **Paradise of God.***

Genesis 2:8-9, NKJ: *8The LORD God planted a garden eastward in Eden, and there He put the man whom He had formed. 9... **The tree of life** was also in the **midst** of the **garden,** and the tree of the knowledge of good and evil.*

Paradise is "the third heaven." The tree of life is in "the middle of the Paradise of God." We also know that this same tree of life is in the "middle of the garden" of Eden (Genesis 2:8-9; 3:22-23). Therefore, Paradise is the Garden of Eden, which is the third heaven. Adam sinned in the Garden of Eden. Therefore, **Adam sinned in the third heaven**. The first sin by Adam was committed in heaven (Genesis 3). Therefore, Jesus' blood had to also reconcile the things in heaven. The logical question is: if Adam sinned in heaven, how did sin get on the earth?

*Genesis 2:15, NKJ: Then the LORD God **took** the man and **put him in the garden of Eden** to tend and keep it.*

*Genesis 3:22-23, NKJ: 22Then the LORD God said, "Behold, the man has become like one of Us, to know good and evil. And now, lest he put out his hand and take also of the tree of life, and eat, and live forever" — 23therefore the LORD God **sent (lit., to drive out, to divorce)** him out of the garden of Eden to till the ground from which he was taken.*

Genesis 2:15 establishes the truth that Adam was **taken** and **"put in the garden of Eden."** The word "took" when referenced by the writer of Hebrews with regards to Enoch means Adam was "translated" into the Garden of Eden, which is the third heaven. After Adam sinned in the third heaven, He was then "driven out" of the third heaven—Eden. Thus, "sin entered the world" through Adam, after he was driven out of the third (world) of heaven.

*Romans 5:12, NKJ: Therefore, just as **through one man sin entered the world**....*

My point is that the Lord had to reconcile the things in heaven because that is where the first Adam and the Devil sinned. I call this "sin in the spirit." It is a serious thing when anyone sins in the spirit, as opposed to sinning in the earth. Whenever a person sins in the spirit (which is heaven, Revelation 4:1-2) a person can forfeit his/her ability to eat of the tree of life.

This may be a reason there are so many "dead"[4] Christians. This may be the reason so many are trying through emotional ecstasy to go to heaven because they were kicked out for sinning in the

---

[4] Compare Revelation 3:1

spirit. The blood of the Lamb is the only way to be reconciled to the heavenly dimensions. God sent His Son to "**reconcile all things** … **things in heaven,** having made **peace through the blood** of His cross." We now sit with Jesus in heaven with the Lord in peace through the Lamb's blood.

*Ephesians 2:4; 6, NKJ: ⁴But God, who is rich in mercy … made us alive together with Christ…⁶and raised us up together and made us sit together in the **heavenly places** in Christ Jesus.*

*Colossians 1:19-20, NKJ: For it pleased the Father that … by Him to **reconcile all things** to Himself, by Him, whether things on earth or **things in heaven,** having made **peace through the blood of His cross.***

Just like the first Adam was taken to the Paradise of God, so likewise, we now sit together in the heavenly places in Christ. There is a key though. You must be in Christ—Head and Body (1 Corinthians 12:12). This is only done "through the blood of His cross." One of the purposes of this heavenly reconciliation is that we can hear the good words of God in our conscience again.

*Ephesians 1:3, NKJ: **Blessed (Gk., eulogetos)** be the God and Father of our Lord Jesus Christ, who has **blessed (Gk., eulogeo)** us with every spiritual blessing **(Gk., eulogia)** in the heavenly places in Christ.*

"Blessed" and "blessing" is a combination of two Greek words— **"eu"** (good or well) and **"logos"** (words or expressed thoughts). We get our English word eulogy from this Greek compound. Eulogy means to speak well over. Remember, earlier in this chapter we showed that the blood of the Lamb speaks "better things." These eulogies are made real by the blood of the Lamb. The heavenly places **in** Christ, through His blood, speak better and good things over us. Here is a good word from the blood of the Lamb—the Lord did not die for you to make you valuable. On the contrary, He paid the price of blood for you because you **are indeed** valuable.

*Matthew 27:3-8, NKJ: ³Then Judas, His betrayer, seeing that He had been condemned… brought back the **thirty pieces of silver** to the chief priests and elders, ⁴… And they said, "What is that to us? You see to it!"*

*5Then he threw down the pieces of silver in the temple ... 6But the chief priests ... said, "It is not lawful to put them into the treasury, because they are **the price of blood."** And they consulted together and bought with them the **potter's field....** 8Therefore that field has been called the **Field of Blood** to this day.*

1 Corinthians 6:20, NKJ: **For you were bought at a price;** *therefore, glorify God in your body and in your spirit, which are God's.*

There is a lot in the verses above. He was sold for thirty pieces of silver. However, it actually "cost" more than that for our salvaging. The Scripture aptly called the "cost" for salvaging us "the price of blood." The price is "thirty pieces of silver. This is what the Zechariah 11:9-13 calls a "goodly price" (KJV) or a "princely price" (NKJV).

The Hebrew definitions for "goodly" or "princely" are amplitude, mantle, expand, great, splendor (see Strong's Concordance). **"Mantle"** points to His blood that covers us. His blood is that **"great"** price. The Lord gives us **"splendor"** through the blood of His Son. The Church is to **"expand"** the Church of the living God, through the blood of the cross.

Finally, the **blood speaks** with an **"amplitude"** that is heard in every creature. The "price" is the blood of God's equal (Jesus), which is also called the "price of blood." **God in the flesh** died for us. We were so valuable to God that **"God manifested in the flesh"** and died for us.

1Timothy 3:16, NKJ: *And without controversy great is the mystery of godliness:* **God** *was manifested in* **the flesh,** *justified in the Spirit, seen by angels, preached among the Gentiles, believed on in the world, received up in glory.*

God birthed Himself in the form of His Son Jesus. God manifested Himself in the flesh to shed His blood for us. He did not only die for us to make us valuable; He died for us because we are indeed valuable. We are that "treasure" that was "hidden in a field" that was worth "all that He [the Lord] has" (Matthew 13:44).

The value of humans was the price of His blood. This is the value the Lord placed on you and me (the value of His very own blood). "For you [us] were bought at a price." His betrayal money was also used to buy the "potter's field" — the "Field of Blood." Jesus said, "the **field** is the **world**" (Matthew 13:38).

The world is a field of blood. Everyone seems to be selling out those whom they do not like. Murder, rape, drug dealing, sexual sins, and the like are prevalent in these times; and it takes the blood of the Lamb to redeem the field of the world that is "struggling" in its own bloodshed (Ezekiel 16:6) and make it a potters' field.

In other words, the Lord is using His blood to redeem those who are guilty of blood. He is then molding the "field" of the world as the potter because He is the Potter (Jeremiah 18:4-11). It took the sweat of God to redeem the World. He resisted sin to the point where blood flowed — the blood of the everlasting covenant.

*Hebrews 13:20, NKJ: Now may the God of peace who brought up our Lord Jesus from the dead, that great Shepherd of the sheep, through the **blood of the everlasting covenant***

*Luke 22:44, NKJ: And being in agony, He prayed more earnestly. Then **His sweat became like great drops of blood** falling down to the ground.*

*Hebrews 12:4, NKJ: You have not yet resisted to **bloodshed**, striving against sin.*

Something **"everlasting"** was established with the blood of Jesus. It is an "everlasting **covenant.**" Jesus prayed so earnestly against sin that His sweat became blood. He strove against sin to the point of bloodshed, before He got abused with beatings, and before blood flowed on the cross. He strove against the sin of mankind in the Garden. Adam sinned in a Garden. Jesus overcame sin in a garden, and He was crucified near a garden (John 18:1; John 19:41).

It was in the Garden of Eden that the Lord said that the curse of "sweat" would be upon Adam for Adam's transgression. It follows that it was in a garden that the Last Adam (Jesus) took on that curse of "sweat" and demolished that curse forever. There is a new covenant. It is **"everlasting"** through the blood of Jesus. We are free from the curse of a nonproductive **earth. "…The profit of the land is for all…" (Ecclesiastes 5:9).** The land must now yield her strength for the children of God (contrast Genesis 4:12 which was implemented because of bloodshed).

Genesis 3:17-19, NKJ: *17Then to Adam He said, "Because you have heeded the voice of your wife and have eaten from the tree of which I commanded you, saying, 'You shall not eat of it': **"Cursed is the ground** for your sake; in toil you shall eat of it all the days of your life. 18Both thorns and thistles it shall bring forth for you, and you shall eat the herb of the field. 19In the sweat of your face you shall eat bread till you return to the ground, for out of it you were taken; for dust you are, and to dust you shall return."*

The ground was cursed because of Adam's sin. It would take his "sweat" to eat bread from the precious earth. The Septuagint (Greek) translation of the Old Testament of this word "sweat" is the same Greek word used by Luke concerning the "sweat" of Jesus that became "as 'clots' of blood."

The link is that the blood-sweat of Jesus redeemed the earth (land) and us from any curse (compare Galatians 3:13; Revelation 22:3). We now have an everlasting covenant which makes us free from the sweat of sin and the sweat of providing for our daily provisions. We "overcame … by the **blood** of the Lamb" (Revelation 12:11).

Chronology of Creation

Genesis 2:18: And the LORD God said, it is not good that the man should be alone; I will make him a help meet for him.

Jesus created all things. "All things were created for Him and by Him" (Colossians 1:16). We also know that Jesus was and is the Word made flesh (John 1:14). It follows that the Word of God can provide insight as to the chronology of creation. There are so many theories concerning the order of creation. However, because Jesus taught us the things of God in simplicity, it appears to me that we can also understand the chronology of God's creation in simplicity of His Word and not with invented ideas.

In the reference above (Genesis 2:18) we see that the man, Adam was already made before God decided to make a "help meet for him" in according to Genesis 2:18. Most have believed that the first help meet that God made after Adam was Mrs. Adam, later called Eve. However, if we go on this premise that the first set of "help meet" was not Eve, then it is established that God also **continued** to create more beings after He made Adam, as it is demonstrated 9n that He continued to create further after day one; after day two; after day three; after day four; after day five; and on the sixth day.

Thus, the concept that God created more creatures other than the ones in Genesis 1:24-25 after Adam should not be difficult to grasp. In fact, sometime in day six, after God mad the male, and before he made the female, God made the original serpent—"a part of the beasts of the field." Here is the chronology relative to the man Adam.

*Genesis 2:4-7: 4These are the generations of the heavens and of the earth when they were created, in the day that the LORD God **made the earth** and **the heavens**, 5and **every plant of the field** before it was in the earth, and **every herb of the field** before it grew: for the LORD God had not caused it to rain upon the earth, and there was **not a man to till the ground.** 6But there went up a mist from the earth and watered the whole face of the ground. 7And **the LORD God formed man of the dust of*** *the ground and* breathed into his nostrils the breath of life; and man became a living soul.

*Genesis 2:18-22: And the LORD God said, it is not good that the man should be alone; I will make him a **help meet** for him. 19**And** out of the ground the LORD God **formed** every **beast of the field,** and every **fowl of the air;** and brought them unto Adam to see what he would call them: and whatsoever Adam called every living creature that was the name thereof. 20And Adam gave names to all cattle, and to the fowl of the air, and to every beast of the field; but for Adam there was not found a help meet for him. 21And the LORD God caused a deep sleep to fall upon Adam, and he slept: and he took one of his ribs and closed up the flesh instead thereof; 22And the rib, which the LORD God had taken from man, **made he a woman**, and brought her unto the man.*

Here are the steps:

1. God made the heavens and the earth.

2. God then made "every plant of the field before it was in the earth and every herb of the field before [they] grew: for the Lord God and not caused it to rain upon the earth and there was no man to [work] the ground."

3. The next chronological step the Lord took in His creating is that He "formed man of the dust of the ground." One of the purposes of the man was to "till the ground," in addition to protecting the Garden of Eden.

4. God then made the first set of "help meet," the beasts of the field and the fowls of the air (both of these are spiritual beings).

5. God then completed His creation with a wife for the man Adam.

Note: At the juncture in God's creation when God made Adam (my step 3 above); God continued to create because there was no female man; and there was no existence of the serpent that was a part of the beasts of the field. **There is a difference between "beasts of** the earth" and "the beast of the field" as we will discover later in this book. Here are the steps again:

God created the heavens and the earth. God called into existence the Light. He then called into existence the firmament in the middle of the waters and divided the waters above the firmament from the waters under the firmament, and so on. God then called for vegetation, herbage, and trees. God then called into existence the sun, moon, and stars. The Lord then called for the creatures of the sea; and afterward, He made the beasts of the **earth.** The Father then made the male man; and then God continued to make other living creatures. God called these additional creations "helpmeet." "And the LORD God said, it is not good that the man should be **alone;** I will make him a help meet for him." The first set of "helpmeets" were beasts of the field, not Mrs. Adam. Here is a brief narrative concerning the first set of "helpmeet."

The man Adam was "alone." Thus, the Lord decided to make a helpmeet for Adam. However, the first helpmeet that the Lord made for Adam was not Mrs. Adam, later called Eve. The first set of "helpmeets" that God made was "every beast of the field" and "every fowl of the air." These beasts of the fields and fowls of the air came after Adam was made and while Adam was in the garden that God planted for him in Eden.

According to Genesis 1:20-25, God already made some fowls of the air and beasts of the "earth" (not beasts of the "field"). Yet, in God's chronology of creation, He continued "further" to create "helpmeet for Adam;" and the first set of which He calls "beasts of the field" and "fowls of the air." Thus, we see that the man, Adam was made before, the beasts of the fields and before the fowls of the air named in Genesis 2:19.

However, these beasts of the field and these fowls of the air were made <u>before</u> Eve — Mrs. Adam. Here is truth that has to be grasped. These beasts of the field are spiritual beings. They are different from the "dumb animals" of the earth. **"Now the serpent was** 'crafty a part of all' the beasts of the field"[5] that was created after Mr. Adam, yet before Mrs. Adam. Adam is senior to the serpent. Thus, mankind in general is senior to the serpent. In fact, it was the male, Adam that named the serpent.

Therefore, in the chronology of God's creation, the Father made the heavens and the earth. He then made the man, Adam. After this, God made some "helpmeet" for the male Adam because the man was "alone." The next order of creation, the "helpmeet," was beasts of the field and fowls of the air. These beasts of the field include the original serpent, Satan. After, God made these beasts of the field and fowls of the air, Adam did not call them a "wife" or "woman." Thus, God continued to "make;" God made the female Adam to be with the male Adam; in fact, the Father "called their name Adam."[6] Therefore, Adam and his wife (being made from Adam) is senior to the serpent.

---

[5] Genesis 3:1 with literal definitions inserted.
[6] Genesis 5:2

God Formed Yet Further

*Genesis 2:19, Septuagint (LXX): And **God formed yet farther** out of the **earth** all the **wild beasts** of the field, and all the birds of the sky, and he brought them to Adam, to see what he would call them, and whatever Adam called any living creature, which was the name of it.*

Jesus is Creator; The Lord is also the Maker of all; and Gods is also the One who forms all. The Septuagint Bible indicate that "God formed **yet farther**" after He completed Adam; and after He placed Adam in the garden that He planted for Adam in Eden. The Septuagint is the Bible that Jesus and all the early apostles used. Jesus quoted it in Matthew 21:16. The writer of Hebrew quoted in Hebrews 10:5. Paul quoted in Galatians 4:27, and so on. Therefore, it is not strange that I use the Septuagint as reference in this book. In the Scripture reference above, we see that "God formed yet farther" after He finished making the male, Adam.

Again, this should not be strange. God continued creating after day one, after day two, after day three, after day four, after day five; and He continued to "make" in day six. In day six God made Mr. Adam; He then made some beasts of the field and some additional fowls of the air; before He "built" Mrs. Adam.

In the words of the Septuagint, "God formed yet farther." The question must then be asked: What or who did God form yet farther? The answers are as follows: The Lord formed the "beasts of field" according to the Hebrew text or "beasts of the earth;" and He formed "the birds of the sky," according to the Greek text of the Old Testament.

*Genesis 2:18-19: [18]And the LORD God said, it is not good that the man should be alone; I will make him a help meet for him. [19]And out of the ground the LORD God formed **every beast of the field,** and every **fowl of the air;** and brought them unto Adam to see what he would call them; and whatsoever Adam called every living creature that was the name thereof.*

In Genesis 2:18, we read that God wanted to make a "help meet" for Adam. In Genesis 2:19. We learn that the first sets of "help meet" that the Lord formed were beasts of the field and fowls of the air. "God formed yet farther ...all the wild beasts of the field, and all the birds of the sky." Note: these beasts of the field and birds of the sky were formed after Mr. Adam; however, they were made before Eve.

Traditionally, some have overlooked the making of the beasts of the field and the second set of the birds of the air as a sequence in the creation process. This oversight has led to many erroneous doctrines concerning Satan that have ascribed more authority to the serpent that what is written. Some have even said that Satan spoke through a serpent in Genesis 3.

The actual truth is that the serpent that spoke in Genesis 3 is actually Satan himself that the beloved John defined as "that 'original' serpent." Paul also made it clear that it was serpent, Satan who "cheated" Eve when Paul compared "Satan" and "his ministers" to the "serpent" and those "false apostles" who "preach another Jesus," impart " 'a different' spirit (the serpent)" and offer "another gospel" (2 Corinthians 11:2-4 with 11:13-15).

*2 Corinthians 11:3-4; 13-15: ³But I fear, lest by any means, as **the serpent** beguiled Eve through his subtlety, so your minds should be corrupted from the simplicity that is in Christ. ⁴For if **he** that comes preaches **another Jesus,** whom we have not preached, or if you receive **another spirit,** which you have not received, or **another gospel,** which you have not accepted, you might well bear with him .... ¹³For such are **false apostles,** deceitful workers, transforming themselves into the apostles of Christ. ¹⁴And no marvel; for **Satan** himself is transformed into an angel of light. ¹⁵Therefore it is no great thing if **his ministers** also be transformed as the ministers of righteousness; whose end shall be according to their works.*

We read in Genesis 3 that it was the same serpent who was "a part of the beasts of the field" that offered Eve **another** understanding of God's command other than what Adam had previously told her. Paul taught the same thing. 'The serpent" is "Satan himself." This serpent Satan was among the beasts of the field that were made after Adam. Yes, when God continued to "form yet farther ...the wild beasts of the field," the serpent, Satan was among these "wild beasts of the field." In other words, the beasts of the field were of a different order that the beasts of the earth in Genesis 1:24-25; 30; and Satan was made at the same time these beasts were made and Satan was a part of them. Satan who is a part of these beasts of the field is who the Bible calls "that 'original' serpent" in the book of The Revelation of Jesus Christ.

"That 'Original' Serpent"

Revelation 12:7-9: *[7]And there was war in heaven: Michael and his angels fought against the dragon; and the dragon fought and his angels, [8]and prevailed not; neither was their place found any more in heaven. [9]And the great dragon was cast out,* **that old serpent,** *called the Devil, and Satan, which deceives the whole world: he was cast out into the earth, and his angels were cast out with him.*

Revelation 12:7-9, NIV: *[7]And there was war in heaven. Michael and his angels fought against the dragon, and the dragon and his angels fought back. [8]But he was* **not strong enough,** *and they lost their place in heaven. [9]The great dragon was hurled down – that ancient serpent called the devil, or Satan, who leads the whole world astray. He was hurled to the earth, and his angels with him.*

Jesus weakened Satan and displaced the Devil out of the world[7] some 2,000 years ago at the cross. Michael the arch angel and his angels also displaced the great dragon and his angels from heaven. The dragon had already been "weakened" by "a Stronger (Jesus)[8] than he (the dragon)." Thus, the dragon was "not strong enough" to resist Michael, as Michael cast the great dragon and his angels out of heaven. When the dragon lost its place in heaven, a revelation of who this great dragon "is" was revealed. The Scriptures says, "The great dragon was cast out, **that old serpent,** called the Devil, and Satan."

The great dragon is called "Satan." This definition is easy to grasp. The great dragon is also called "the Devil." This definition is also not hard to comprehend. However, when it is also called "that old serpent" there is more to this name than meets the eye. Here is an understanding. The Greek word for **"old"** literally means **"original"** (NT: #744, Strong's Concordance, etc.). Thus, the great dragon is "that **'original'** serpent." Therefore, here is a logical question: where in the Bible can we find this "original" serpent? The only original serpent that I am aware of is the original serpent that tempted Mr. and Mrs. Adam in Genesis 3. Yes, the serpent

---

[7] John 12:31
[8] Luke 11:22

identified in Genesis 3:1 is "that **'original'** serpent" that the Lord made. The Lord made the serpent(s) — "'a part of' the beasts of the field" — after Mr. Adam, but before Mrs. Adam (later called Eve). This is the same serpent that tempted Eve.

*2 Corinthians 11:3: But I fear, lest by any means, as **the serpent** beguiled Eve through his subtlety, so your minds should be corrupted from the simplicity that is in Christ.*

Many have invented doctrines concerning the serpent in Genesis 3. They have said that it was a natural serpent (beast of the earth) that the Devil spoke through. However, the Scripture teaches that the serpent was "a part of" the beast of the field. Paul declared that it was "the serpent" that "beguiled Eve." Therefore, the serpent that deceived Mrs. Adam was a different order than the natural serpent. The serpent in the garden was of an order of cherubs that the Lord created in the garden to originally help Adam before some of them were eventually cursed by God; and they can talk.

*Genesis 3:1: Now the serpent was **more** subtle **than** any beast of the field which the LORD God had made. And **he said** unto the woman, Yes, has God said, you shall not eat of every tree of the garden?*

The two words "more … than" highlighted in Genesis 3:1 above, is the Hebrew word "MKL." This Hebrew word is a compound of two words "Min" and "KoL." "Min" literally means "a part of," "out of," "from," etc. "Kol" means "every," "all," "whole," etc. Therefore, "the serpent was subtle **'a part of all'** the beasts of the field." Or "the serpent was subtle **'out of all'** the beasts of the field." The serpent was indeed dragon or a snake; however, it was not a natural snake. This serpent was, in reality, a great dragon, called Satan and the Devil that could also **speak.** It follows that we can now see why John branded Satan as "that 'original' serpent called the Devil and Satan." The serpent was "a part of" the beasts of the field that was originally made to help Adam.

With that said, I will now conclude this chapter with a vision I saw of one of these dragons, called the false prophet in the early years of the 1990s – early one morning – between 3-5 AM. My wife and I were in a season of intensified prayer. We were continually interceding starting in the nights and finishing deep into the early mornings. One morning after praying most of the night into the morning, after we went to sleep, immediately I was in a vision. I saw a red (komodo-like) dragon; and I was fighting this dragon in a heat of a battle. I wrestled this red dragon and forced it out the sky to the ground. I then descended from the heavenly to investigate to make sure he (it) was defeated. My clothes were ripped up as a result of the intense fighting with this beast (compare 1 Corinthians 15:32).

As I descended, to make sure he (it) was defeated, the red dragon began to pursue me again. I ascended again to the heavens as he pursued me. In his pursuit of me I turned towards him to fight, and fire came out of my mouth and devoured him (Compare Revelation 11:5, Jeremiah 23:29). The beast then fell to the ground, again, as dead, however he was not. As I descended from the heavenly, again, I saw my wife going towards the dragon to throw some sort of solid foam on the beast. As she was about to do this, I called out to her and said," Judy, he is not dead as he may appear." As I said this to my wife, the beast stood up; and to my amazement the red dragon had mutated into a man with ram's horns. His appearance was that of a man[9] or an angel, but he had two huge horns like a male lamb. The horns started from his ears and temples and reached down towards his cheek area. At this sight, the vision ended.

The beast that I encountered in the vision represents the beast identified in Revelation 13:11 as "another beast;" and in Revelation 19:20 he is called "the false prophet." I later learned that the Septuagint called the beasts of the field, "wild beasts of the field." The Greek word translated as "wild beasts" is the same Greek word used of "the beast" that is ascending out of the bottomless pit" in Revelation 11:7. It also the same word used for "another beast" in Revelation 13:11, and so on. In Revelation 13:11, we get a

---

[9] The man with the ram's horns in the vision looked like a prominent TV preacher.

glimpse of the meaning of "**another beast**" that is in reality a "dragon."

*Revelation 13:11: And I beheld **another beast** coming up out of the earth; and he had two horns like a lamb, and he spoke **as a dragon**.*

The Scripture says this beast **speaks as** a dragon. The word **as** is the Greek word "hos" (hoce), which means **"which how."** "Hos" is from a root word that means who, which, what, that (Strong's #5613, #3739). So, this phrase could read: "he spoke **which how** a dragon;" meaning he **"which"** is a dragon spoke **"how?"** He spoke **"as"** a dragon! In other words, he spoke **as** a dragon because, in reality, he **is** a dragon. The serpent is also called a "great dragon," and therefore a "beast" of the field like the beasts of Revelation 13; and the Lord made these wild beasts of the field after Adam.

Beasts of the Field-Fowls of the Air

Genesis 2:18-19: *18And the LORD God said, it is not good that the man should be alone; I will make him a help meet for him. 19And out of the ground the LORD God formed **every beast of the field,** and every fowl of the air; and brought them unto Adam to see what he would call them: and whatsoever Adam called every living creature that was the name thereof.*

*Genesis 3:1: Now **the serpent was more subtle than any beast of the field** which the LORD God had made. And he said unto the woman, Yes, has God said, you shall not eat of every tree of the garden?*

Jesus, the Lord, was interested in making a "helpmeet" for Adam. In Genesis 2:18, we read that the Lord desired to make "a helpmeet" for Adam because Adam was alone in the garden. The first "helpmeet" that the Lord made were "beasts of the field" and "fowls of the air." The serpent was "a part of" these beasts of the field. Or the serpent was "out of" the beasts of the field. These "beasts of the **field**" were created **after** the "beasts of the **earth**" in Genesis 1:24-25; 30.

As God continue to create in the various **days** listed in Genesis 1, so likewise the Lord continued to create in day six after He placed Adam in the Garden of Eden. The Lord continued to make the beast of the field, the fowls of the air; and afterward, He later "built" the woman.

With that said, there are a couple of Hebrew words that I will highlight that are translated as "beast" in Genesis. There is "bhema" – "beasts," or "cattle;" and there is "chay" – "living creatures." "Bhema" is translated as "cattle" in Genesis 3:14, and as "beasts" in Genesis 7:1-2. "Chay" is translated as "living creatures" as seen in Ezekiel 1 and Ezekiel 10. The beasts of the earth are cattle and other beasts on the earth that are muted. In fact, the literal definition for "bhema" is "dumb beast" (see OT: #929, Strong's Concordance). They cannot speak with languages as humans unless God opens their mouth to speak (2 Peter 2:16). The beasts of the field are of another order, they can speak; and in the teaching of the Scriptures some of these "beasts of the field" are also cherubs.

*Genesis 3:1: Now **the serpent** was subtle **'a part of the living creature'** **of the field** which the LORD God had made. And he said unto the woman, Yes, has God said, you shall not eat of every tree of the garden?*

*Ezekiel 1:5-8: ⁵Also out of the midst thereof came the likeness of four **living creatures.** And this was their appearance; they had the **likeness** of a **man.** ⁶And everyone had **four faces,** and everyone had **four wings.** ⁷And their feet were **straight feet;** and the sole of their feet was like the sole of a calf's foot: and they sparkled like the color of burnished brass. ⁸And they had the hands of a man under their wings on their four sides; and they four had their faces and their wings.*

In Ezekiel 1:4-5 we see that there were four "living creatures" that appeared out of a great cloud. This word "living creatures" is the Hebrew word "chay" also translated as "beast" in Genesis 2:19 and genesis 3:1. It follows that the "beasts of the field" in Genesis 2:19 and genesis 3:1 may also be translated as "'living creatures' of the field." Yes, the "beasts" in Genesis 2:19 and Genesis 3:1 are actually "'**living creatures'** of the field;" that is, they are of a higher order than the "'living creatures' of the earth" in Genesis 1:24-25; 30. In Ezekiel 10, the living creatures are identified as cherubs.

*Ezekiel 10:1-2; 20-22: ¹Then I looked, and behold, in the firmament that was above the head of the **cherubim** there appeared over them as it were a sapphire stone, as the appearance of the likeness of a throne. ²And he spoke unto the man clothed with linen, and said, Go in between the wheels, even under the **cherub,** and fill thine hand with coals of fire from between the **cherubim,** and scatter them over the city. And he went in in my sight .... ²⁰This is the **living creature** that I saw under the God of Israel by the river of Chebar; and I knew that they were the **cherubim.** ²¹Every one had **four faces apiece,** and everyone four wings; and the likeness of the hands of a man was under their wings. ²²And the likeness of their faces was the same faces which I saw by the river of Chebar, their appearances and themselves: they went everyone straight forward.*

Ezekiel defined the "living creatures" as "cherubs." These cherubs all have "four faces apiece." "That 'original' serpent" also appears to have four faces."

Revelation 12:14: *And to the woman were given two wings of a great eagle, that she might fly into the wilderness, into her place, where she is nourished for a time, and times, and half a time, from the* **face of the serpent.**

Note: there are four names for the great dragon; and it appears that a "face" coincides with each name. The names are these: "great dragon," "that 'original' serpent," "Devil," and "Satan." We see in Revelation 12:14 that the serpent has a "face." The woman (natural Israel and/or "the Israel of God (the Church)) was protected from the "face of the serpent." It appears logical through the Holy Spirit that the "great dragon also has a "face;" Satan also has a "face;" and the Devil also has a "face."

Thus, Satan has four faces like the cherubs each have four faces. These cherubs are called "living creatures" that is also translated as "beasts;" the same word used for the serpent—"'a part of' the beasts of the field" in Genesis 3:1. The serpent in Genesis 3:1 was not a natural serpent. It was a spiritual cherub with four faces which coincides to its four names. This serpent could speak, as do seraphs cherubs.

Isaiah 6:1-4: [1]*In the year that king Uzziah died I saw also the Lord sitting upon a throne, high and lifted up, and his train filled the temple.* [2]*Above it stood the* **seraphim:** *each one had* **six wings;** *with twain he covered his face, and with twain he covered his feet, and with twain he did fly.* [3]*And one* **cried** *unto another, and* **said, holy, holy, holy, is the LORD** *of hosts: the whole earth is full of his glory.* [4]*And the posts of the door moved at the* **voice** *of him that cried, and the house was filled with smoke.*

Unlike cherubs that have four wings, these seraphs (lit., fiery ones) have six wings. These six-winged creatures are also seen in Revelation 4. In Revelation 4 they cry practically the same thing **"holy, holy, holy is the LORD ...."** These Scriptures coupled together shows that the living creatures in Revelation 4 are seraphs and not cherubs.

Revelation 4:6-8: [6]*And before the throne there was a sea of glass like unto crystal: and in the midst of the throne, and round about the throne, were **four beasts** full of eyes before and behind.* [7]*And the first beast was like a **lion,** and the second beast like a **calf,** and the third beast had a face as a **man,** and the fourth beast was like a **flying eagle.** [8]And the four beasts had each of them **six wings** about him; and they were full of eyes within: and they rest not day and night, **saying, Holy, holy, holy, Lord God** Almighty, which was, and is, and is to come.*

As can be seen these seraphs had "six wings" like those of Isaiah 6. These **"beasts" (or lit., living ones)** can speak as seen in the fact that the living ones were **"saying."** Yes, there are living creatures in the invisible that speaks; and yes, the serpent is like some of these living creatures. This makes them of a different order than natural beasts of the earth. There is a difference between "beasts of the earth" (fleshly animals); and the beasts of the field (which also points to spirit creatures) in the invisible. This is also seen in the prophetic eagle in mid-heaven that spoke.

*Revelation 8:13, NIV: As I watched, I heard an **eagle** that was flying in **midair** call out in a **loud voice:** "Woe! Woe! Woe to the inhabitants of the earth, because of the trumpet blasts about to be sounded by the other three angels!"*

The NIV[10] correctly translate the Greek texts[11] in Revelation 8:13. The "eagle … call out with a loud voice: Woe! Woe! Woe …." This should not be strange. Why? Because when God continued to "form yet farther" in Genesis 2:18-19, He also made some additional "fowls of the air." These fowls of the air are different from the typical ones cited in Genesis 1: 21; 30. The fowls of the air that were formed in Genesis 2:19 were also originally made to be a helpmeet for Adam. However, some of them also fell. This is seen when Jesus likens some of the "fowls of the air" to Satan, which I believe is a corporate Satan, since "fowls" are plural.

---

[10] New International Version
[11] The Majority texts (or Byzantine Texts) of over 5,000 manuscripts and the Alexandrian texts all have "eagle" in these oldest texts.

Genesis 2:18-19: [18]*And the LORD God said, it is not good that the man should be alone; I will make him a help meet for him.* [19]*And out of the ground the LORD God formed every beast of the field, **and** every **fowl of the air;** and brought them unto Adam to see what he would call them: and whatsoever Adam called every living creature that was the name thereof.*

Mark 4:3-4; 15: [3]*Hearken; Behold, there went out a sower to sow:* [4]*And it came to pass, as he sowed, some fell by the wayside, and the **fowls of the air** came and devoured it up....* [15]*And these are they by the wayside, where the word is sown; but when they have heard, **Satan** comes immediately, and taketh away the word that was sown in their hearts.*

Jesus in the verses above in simile equated "fowls (plural) of the air" to Satan (singular). As we will see in the next chapter, Jesus taught that there is a corporate Satan. In other words, all the angels that follow Satan are also called "Satan."[12] In Genesis 2:18-19, we have learned that the beasts of the field points to spiritual beings of which is the serpent. It follows that the "fowls of the air" in Genesis 2:19 also points to spiritual beings. This is not far fetch; because in Revelation 8:13, we see that there are spiritual eagle(s) that "fly in midair" speaking in "a loud voice." Was this the eagle seraph of Revelation 4:7 flying with its six wings? Or was this some other eagle in mid-heaven speaking? This point is this there are other living creatures that were created to help Adam before Mrs. Adam was built.

---

[12] Matthew 12

Corporate Leviathan — Seven, Ten and Tail

Matthew 12:22; 24-26: *[22]Then was brought unto him one possessed with a devil, blind, and dumb: and he healed him, insomuch that the blind and dumb both spoke and saw…. [24]But when the Pharisees heard it, they said, this fellow doth not cast out devils, but by Beelzebub the prince of the devils. [25]And Jesus knew their thoughts, and said unto them, every kingdom divided against itself is brought to desolation; and every city or house divided against itself shall not stand:* *[26]And if **Satan cast out Satan**, he is divided against himself; how shall then his kingdom stand?*

Jesus healed a person possessed with a devil. However, instead of the Pharisees rejoicing that a person had been healed, they began to blaspheme Jesus and the Holy Spirit in Jesus. In addition, Jesus' response was also very insightful. In Jesus' response, He declared that "Satan" was in essence a corporate entity. That is, the angels and demons that follow Satan (lit., satanas) are also called "Satan" (lit., satanan). There is a difference between "satanas" (Satan himself) and "satanan" (the corporate Satan).

"The Pharisees … said this fellow doth not cast out **devils,** but by **Beelzebub** the prince of the devils." Jesus responded by saying, "and if **Satan** cast out **Satan,** he is divided against himself; how shall his kingdom stand?" There is Satan the prince of devils; and there is Satan, the many devils. This shows that there is a corporate Satan. The corporate Satan is seen in leviathan with its heads; it is seen in the great dragon with its seven heads, ten horns and its tail. Our Lord Jesus also demonstrated this truth in the parable of the Sower.

Mark 4:3-4; 15: *[3]Hearken; behold, there went out a sower to sow:* *[4] And it came to pass, as he sowed, some fell by the wayside, and the **fowls of the air** came and devoured it up…. [15]And these are they by the wayside, where the word is sown; but when they have heard, **Satan** cometh immediately, and taketh away the word that was sown in their hearts.*

The "fowls (plural) of the air" are called "Satan." Thus, Satan is a corporate entity. In Revelation 12 we learn that "the great dragon, that 'original' serpent called the Devil and Satan" has seven heads and ten horns. We learned earlier that the serpent also had four faces; and the original serpent also has a "tail." How can the serpent have seven heads, yet only four faces? It appears to me that the seven head points to the corporate heads (ruling angels) that are also called Satan. Their purpose is to continue to test and tempt the saints of the living God.

*Revelation 12:3-4: 3And there appeared another wonder in heaven; and behold a great red dragon, having **seven** heads and **ten** horns, and seven crowns upon his heads. 4And his **tail** drew the third part of the stars of heaven and did cast them to the earth ….*

*Psalm 74:14: You break the **heads** of **leviathan** in pieces and gave him to be meat to the people inhabiting the wilderness.*

*Job 41:1; 34: 1Canst you draw out **leviathan** with a hook? Or his tongue with a cord which you let down … 34He beholds all high things: **he is a king** over all the children of pride.*

*Isaiah 27:1: In that day, the LORD with his 'severe' and great and strong sword shall punish **leviathan the piercing serpent,** even **leviathan** that **crooked serpent;** and he shall slay the **dragon** that is in the sea.*

We see in the references above that leviathan is "the piercing serpent," "crooked serpent" and "the dragon." Leviathan is also "a king;" and he has "heads." The book of Revelation reveals that this dragon, leviathan, is the great dragon, Satan and leviathan has "seven heads." The great dragon has four names (natures or faces), seven heads, ten horns, and a tail. The original serpent has seven, ten and tail.

It has "seven heads" — angels that other angels and the leopard beast submit to. The seven spirit heads (they are not flesh and blood entities) could be listed as follows: beginnings, authorities, world-governments, spirits of hurts (also linked to poverty), powers, thrones, and lords (Ephesians 6:12, Ephesians 1:21, Colossians 1:16). It has "ten horns" — invisible "world-strengths (powers)" and the ten visible kings of the leopard beast's rule. It has a tail — the false prophet, the spirit, which teaches lies in and through the "many false prophets." The serpent is **not** omnipresent; it is **not** omnipotent; it is **not** omniscience. However, it is a corporate entity; and thus, we have to be aware of the wiles of the Devil. **Satan's seven heads** are categorized in Scriptures as **follows: beginnings, powers, authorities, world-governments, spiritual hurts upon-heaven, thrones, and lords (Ephesians 1:21, Ephesians 6:12, Colossians 1:16).**

There are indeed many **invisible "thrones** … dominions …principalities … 'authorities'"** that were created by Jesus and for Jesus. "For by him were all things created, that are in heaven, and that are in earth, visible and **invisible,** whether they be **thrones,** or **dominions,** or **principalities,** or **powers (lit., authorities):** all things were created by him, and for him" (Colossians 1:16).

"Thrones" are the seats of "kings" who are **"crowned."** The dragon had "seven heads … and seven **crowns** upon his heads." Since the dragon's heads were crowned, they are also "kings" (visible[13] and invisible). The corporate Satan has "seven heads" that roam through the earth as "Satan." An example of an enemy angel that is a king is the angel death — "king of terrors."

Job 18:11-14: [11]*Terrors shall make him afraid on every side and shall drive him to his feet.* [12]*His strength shall be hunger-bitten, and destruction shall be ready at his side.* [13]*It shall devour the strength of his skin: even the firstborn of death shall devour his strength.* [14]*His confidence shall be rooted out of his tabernacle, and it shall bring him to the king of terrors.*

*Revelation 6:8: And I looked and behold a pale horse: and his name that sat on him was **Death**, and Hell followed with him. And power was given unto them over the fourth part of the earth, to kill with sword, and with hunger, and with death, and with the beasts of the earth.*

In the reference above we see that there is a **"king** of terrors." This "king" also has a "firstborn." This firstborn is identified as "the firstborn of death." Job also identified the firstborn of death with

---

[13] The dragon seven heads also represent the seven heads (seven kings) of the beast in Revelation 13 and Revelation 17.

hunger ("hunger-bitten") and "destruction." Revelation 6:8 states that the four facets of Death and Hell are: the "sword," "hunger," "death" and "beasts of the earth" (i.e., any beasts of the earth that kills humans). Death is indeed a king, one of the heads of the dragon. However, even this king of terror is totally subjected to Jesus. **Jesus "destroyed him that 'held' the power of death that is the Devil; and delivers them who through fear were all their lifetime subject to 'slavery'"** (Hebrews 2:14-15).

With that said, here are some of the other kings that are heads or horns of the corporate Satan. There is also "king Heylel" — the king of (mystery) Babylon (Isaiah 14:12). There is an invisible "'chief' of Persia" or the invisible "kings of Persia" (Daniel 10:13). There is the **"spirit** of the **kings** of the Medes." The fact that this "spirit" is related to the many "kings of Medes" also makes this spirit a "king" (Jeremiah 51:11). The corporate dragon also had "ten horns."[14] Horns are symbolic of a kingdom, power, or strength. Horns are used to symbolize war or power in war, and so on.

Deuteronomy 33:17, NKJ: His glory is like a firstborn bull, and his horns like the horns of the wild ox; together with them he shall push the peoples to the ends of the earth; they are the ten thousands of Ephraim, and they are the thousands of Manasseh.

Daniel 8:3; 5-7, NKJ: ³Then I lifted my eyes and saw, and there, standing beside the river, was a ram which had two horns, and the two horns were high; but one was higher than the other, and the higher one came up last…. ⁵And as I was considering, suddenly a male goat came from the west, across the surface of the whole earth, without touching the ground; and the goat had a notable horn between his eyes. ⁶Then he came to the ram that had two horns, which I had seen standing beside the river, and ran at him with furious power. ⁷And I saw him confronting the ram; he was moved with rage against him, attacked the ram, and broke his two horns. There was no power in the ram to withstand him ….

As we can see in both references above horns represents "power" to "push" and that "broken horns" means "no power." Therefore,

---

[14] The dragon ten horns also point the ten horns of the beast that represents ten kings with their kingdoms (Revelation 13; Revelation 17).

the ten horns of the dragon represent ten powers that attempts to "push" keep humanity in a defeated state through spiritual warfare. Since horns are symbol of "power," it appears to me that the horns represent the corporate "world-strengths" of Satan that "use strength" to "hold" unsaved and weak people to the "world."

*Ephesians 6:12: For we do not wrestle against flesh and blood, but against principalities, against powers, against **the rulers of the darkness of this age,** against spiritual hosts of wickedness in the heavenly places.*

The phrase "rulers of the darkness of this age" literally reads "'world-strengths' or 'world-governments' of the darkness of this age." The word "rulers" is the Greek compound "kosmoskrator" which means world-governments, or world-holders, or world-strengths, world-powers, or system holders, system-strengths, system-government, system-rule, etc. For what are some of the works of these world-governments or system-holders?

It seems to me that these are part of the corporate Satan that "use strength" to "hold" people to the "system" of the "world," sometimes through governmental systems These spirits also use their horns (power) to war against the souls of humanity with different types of lusts in an effort to keep them bound to the world. These lusts are the **"lust of the flesh, the lust of the eyes and the 'boastings about goods'"** ("conspicuous consumption").

*1 Peter 2:11, NKJ: Beloved, I beg you as sojourners and pilgrims, abstain from fleshly **lusts** which **war against the soul.***

1 John 2:15-17, NKJ: ¹⁵*Do not love the **world** or the **things** in the world. If anyone loves the world, the love of the Father is not in him.* ¹⁶*For all that is in the world – the **lust of the flesh,** the **lust of the eyes,** and the **pride of life** – is not of the Father but is of the world.* ¹⁷*And the world is passing away, and the lust of it; but he who does the will of God abides forever.*

Peter stated that lust war against the soul. Lust is also identified as "things in the world." We also learn that there are "world-holders." These "world-holders" are part of the corporate Satan demons used to hold people to the "things in the world." Thus, once a believer is placed "in Christ," Jesus, through faith in Jesus, we "escape **the corruption** that is **in the world** through **lust.**" (2 Peter 1:14). Through the love that the Father has poured into our hearts by the Holy Spirit we overcome the ten horns of the enemy. With that said, we will now conclude this chapter with the "tail of the dragon."

Revelation 12:3-4: ³*And there appeared another wonder in heaven; and behold **a great red dragon,** having **seven** heads and **ten** horns, and seven crowns upon his heads.* ⁴*And his **tail** drew the third part of the stars of heaven and did cast them to the earth ....*

*Isaiah 9:15, NKJ: The elder and honorable, he is the head; **the prophet** who teaches lies, he is **the tail.***

The dragon is a corporate entity. As we have seen, its seven heads can represent seven head angels; its ten[15] horns can represent the corporate horns of trial and temptation that uses strengths to keep some in the world system through lusts. It follows that the tail of the dragon is also a corporate entity. **The tail of the dragon is "the prophet who teaches lies."** In Revelation 13:11-13 we learn of "another beast" that performed great signs. In Revelation 19:20, we learn that the beast identified as "another beast" is in reality "the false prophet." We also see this same false prophet in Revelation 16:13-14. This "false prophet" is the tail of the dragon; and it is a **spirit** as we will see in a moment.

*Revelation 13:11; 13: ¹¹And I beheld **another beast** coming up out of the earth; and he had two horns like a lamb, and he spoke as a dragon ....* ¹³*And **he doeth great wonders** ....*

*Revelation 19:20: And the beast was taken, and with him **the false prophet that wrought miracles before him** ....*

---

[15] Ten (10) is the number that represents trials and temptations in the Scriptures (see Numbers 14:22).

*1 John 4:1: Beloved, believe not every **spirit,** but try the spirits whether they are of God: because **many false prophets** are gone out into the world.*

Isaiah stated that the "tail" is "the false prophet who teaches lies." This tail or false prophet is also a **"spirit"** — "do not believe every **spirit,** but test the **spirits,** whether they are of God; because **many false prophets** have gone out into the **world.**" Thus, the dragon's tail is also a symbol of "the spirit" named "the false prophet" that uses the many false prophets to deceive unstable souls and the world by lies.

These "lies" ranges from pseudo signs (lying signs), to preaching the "world" and "the lie" itself.[16] "The lie" is defined as those who worship the creation (created things) instead or more than the Creator. These are those "who changed the truth of God into a lie and **worshipped and served the creature more than the Creator,** who is blessed forever. Amen!" (Romans 1:25). With that is said, let us look at some examples of work of the tail of the dragon.

1. Examples of a pseudo signs of the false prophet:

Revelation 13:11; 13; 15: [11]*And I beheld **another beast** coming up out of the earth; and he had two horns like a lamb, and he spoke as a dragon …. [13]And **he doeth great wonders,** so **that he makes fire come down from heaven** on the earth in the sight of men …. [15]And he had power to give life (lit., spirit) unto the **image** of the beast, that the image of the beast should **both speak,** and cause that as many as would not worship the image of the beast should **be killed.***

Revelation 16:13-14 : [13]*And I saw three unclean spirits like frogs come out of the mouth of the dragon, and out of the mouth of the beast, and out of **the mouth of the false prophet.** [14]**For they are the spirits of devils, working miracles,** which go forth unto the kings of the earth and of the whole world, to gather them to the battle of that great day of God Almighty.*

---

[16] Note: "the lie" is discussed in detail in some of my other titles—*Sexual Healing, The False Prophet, Alias, Another Beast, The Work of Lawlessness Revealed,* etc.

2. The false prophet teaches to love the world system.

*1 John 4:1; 5: ¹Beloved, believe not every **spirit,** but try the spirits whether they are of God: because **many false prophets** are gone out into the world …. ⁵They are of the world: therefore, **speak them of the world** and the world hears them.*

*1 John 2:15-17, NKJ: ¹⁵Do not love the **world** or the **things** in the world. **If anyone loves the world, the love of the Father is not in him.** ¹⁶For all that is in the world – the **lust of the flesh,** the **lust of the eyes,** and the **pride of life** – is not of the Father but is of the world. ¹⁷And the world is passing away, and the lust of it; but he who does the will of God abides forever.*

3. The "false prophet," alias, "another beast" teach people to follow the beast and its system of merchandising. As indicated in this book, the "another beast" in Revelation 13:11-13 is the false prophet in Revelation 19:20 and Revelation 16:13. Thus, for ease of reading, I will insert the term "the false prophet" for **"he"** which refers to "another beast," in the reference below.

*Revelation 19:20: And the beast was taken, and with him the **false prophet that wrought miracles** before him, **with which he deceived** them that had received the mark of the beast, and them that worshipped his image. These both were cast alive into a lake of fire burning with brimstone.*

*Revelation 13:11-18: ¹¹And I beheld **another beast** coming up out of the earth; and he had two horns like a lamb, and he spoke as a dragon. ¹²And [**the false prophet**] exercises all the power of the first beast before him and causes the earth and them which dwell therein to worship the first beast, whose deadly wound was healed. ¹³And [**the false prophet**] doeth great wonders, so that [**the false prophet**] makes fire come down from heaven on the earth in the sight of men, ¹⁴And deceives them that dwell on the earth by the means of those miracles which [**the false prophet**] had power to do in the sight of the beast; saying to them that dwell on the earth, that **they should make an image to the beast,** which had the wound by a sword, and did live. ¹⁵And [**the false prophet**] had power to give **life (lit., spirit)** unto the image of the beast, that the image* *of the beast should both speak, and cause that as many as would not worship the image of the beast should be killed.* ¹⁶*And [the false prophet] causes all, both small and great, rich, and poor, free and bond, to receive a mark in their right hand, or in their foreheads:* ¹⁷*And that no man might buy or sell, save he that had the mark, or the name of the beast, or the number of his name.* ¹⁸*Here is wisdom. Let him that has understanding count the number of the beast: for it is the number of a man (lit., because of man); and his number is Six hundred threescore and six.*

4. The false prophet teaches "the lie" — speaking from one's own, and practicing sexual impurity (adultery, same sex practices, fornication, etc.):

John 8:44: *You are of your father the devil, and the lusts of your father you will do. He was a murderer from the beginning, and abode not in the truth, because there is no truth in him. When he speaks a lie (lit., the lie), he speaks of (lit., from) his own: for he is a liar, and the father of it.*

Jeremiah 28:15-17: ¹⁵*Then said the prophet Jeremiah unto Hananiah the prophet, hear now, Hananiah; the LORD has not sent thee; but you make this people to trust in a lie.* ¹⁶*Therefore thus says the LORD; Behold, I will cast you from off the face of the earth: this year you shalt die, because you have taught rebellion against the LORD.* ¹⁷*So Hananiah the prophet died the same year in the seventh month.*

Jeremiah 29:21-23: ²¹*Thus says the LORD of hosts, the God of Israel, of Ahab the son of Kolaiah, and of Zedekiah the son of Maaseiah, which prophesy a lie unto you in my name ....* ²²*And of them shall be taken up a curse by all the captivity of Judah which are in Babylon, saying, The LORD make you like Zedekiah and like Ahab, whom the king of Babylon roasted in the fire;* ²³*because they have committed villainy in Israel, and have committed adultery with their neighbors' wives, and have spoken lying words in my name, which I have not commanded them; even I know, and am a witness, says the LORD.*

We see above that false prophets can perform great signs; they also preach the love of the world and the things therein; they are also liars. That is, they speak from themselves. They go around with claims that God has spoken to them; yet on the contrary, the Father has not spoken to them or sent them to prophesy. In Revelation 12:4 we read that the corporate dragon's "**tail** drew the third part of **the stars of heaven and** did cast them to the earth." According to the Scriptures, the stars of heaven are Abraham's seed. Thus, the false prophet's purpose is to cast as many of God's people as it can to the earth by "plastic" or "molded" words. Why? In the "earthly" dimension saints can become less powerful.

Genesis 15:5: ⁵*And He brought [Abram] forth abroad, and said, look now toward heaven, and* **tell the stars,** *if you be able to number them: and He said unto him,* **so shall thy seed be.**

Hebrews 11:11-12: ¹¹*Through faith also Sara herself received strength to conceive seed and was delivered of a child when she was past age ....* ¹²*Therefore sprang there even of one, and him as good as dead, so many as* **the stars of the sky** *in multitude ....*

Revelation 6:12-13: ¹²*And I beheld when he had opened the sixth seal, and, lo, there was a great earthquake ....*¹³*And* **the stars of heaven** *fell unto the earth ....*

Revelation 12:3-4: ³*And there appeared another wonder in heaven ...* **a great red dragon,** *having* **seven** *heads and* **ten** *horns ....* ⁴*And his* **tail** *drew* **the third part of the stars of heaven and** *did cast them to the earth.*

The corporate Satan is an entity that is targeting the woman (the corporate Church); her seed (Jesus and the corporate male child); and the posterity of Abraham (the stars of heaven), the general assembly. He is using its "seven, ten and tail" to make war against the Lamb, the woman and "her seed." However, as it is written, the Lamb have already overcome them; and we are overcoming them through the blood and the authority of the Lamb—Jesus, the Christ.

Revelation 12:10-11: ¹⁰*And I heard a loud voice saying in heaven, now is come salvation, and strength, and the kingdom of our God, and the power of his Christ: for the accuser of our brethren is cast down, which accused them before our God day and night.* ¹¹**And they overcame him** *by the blood of the Lamb, and by the word of their testimony; and they loved not their lives unto the death.*

According to John, we overcome Satan, including but limited to the corporate Satan, by the blood of the Lamb (Jesus); we overcome Satan by what we speak (the words of our testimony about Jesus); and we should not love our lives (lit. soul) above Jesus. The Bible also show other Scriptures where we have already been made victorious over the corporate Satan ("satanan"). Let us look at those also.

Matthew 12:22; 24-26: 22Then was brought unto him one possessed with a devil, blind, and dumb: and he healed him, insomuch that the blind and dumb both spoke and saw…. 24But when the Pharisees heard it, they said, this fellow doth not cast out devils, but by **Beelzebub the prince of the devils** *…. 26And if* **Satan (lit., satanas) cast out Satan (lit., satanan)**, *he is divided against himself; how shall then his kingdom stand?*

Luke 10:18: And he said unto them, I beheld Satan (lit., satanan) as lightning 'falling' from heaven.

Romans 16:20: And the God of peace shall bruise Satan (lit., satanan) under your feet **shortly (lit., swiftly).** *The grace of our Lord Jesus Christ [be] with you. Amen*

Remember as previously indicated, Jesus' response to the Pharisees in Matthew 12:26, recited above, was also very insightful. In Jesus' response, He declared that "Satan" was in essence a corporate entity. That is, the angels and demons that follow Satan (lit., satanas) are also called "Satan" (lit., satanan). There is a difference between "satanas" (Satan himself) and "satanan" (the corporate Satan (demons)). This "parsing" of words is important to know relative to the Church's victory already realized in Jesus. The corporate Satan (lit., "satanan") is continually falling out of heaven every time the Church uses the name of Jesus to cast out the Devil and his demons. The God of peace also bruise Satan (lit., "satanan") under our feet swiftly. Yes, God also bruises under our feet the corporate "satanan" swiftly!

Where did God Make the Serpent?

*Genesis 2:7-9: 7And the LORD God formed man of the dust of the **ground and** breathed into his nostrils the breath of life; and man became a living soul. 8And the LORD **God planted a garden eastward in Eden;** and **there** he **put** the man whom he had formed. 9And out of the ground made the LORD God to grow every tree that is pleasant to the sight, and good for food, **the tree of life** also in the midst of the garden, and the tree of knowledge of good and evil.*

The Lord formed the man, Adam. The Lord then planted a garden in Eden for Adam; and "there He **put** (lit., place) the man whom he formed." In was also stated that God eventually "allowed" Adam to "stay" in the Garden. This is important to know, because it was after Adam was allowed to stay in the garden that the Lord made the beasts of the field and the fowls of the air from the ground related to the garden.

*Genesis 2:15: And the LORD God **took** the man and **put** him into the Garden of Eden to dress it and to keep it.*

In Genesis 2:8, Adam was "put" ("suwm") in the garden. In Genesis 2:15, Adam was "allowed to stay" ("yanach") in the garden. Genesis 2:15 also stated that the Lord "took" the man when he was "put" in the garden. This word "took" is the same word that is used where it is written that "God took [Enoch]" (Genesis 2:21-24). The word "took" is defined in the New Testament as "translated" (Hebrew 11:15).

Therefore, Adam was "translated" from the earth to the "garden in Eden;" and was thus "allowed to stay" after God "translated" ("took") him there. During Adam's stay in the garden is when the Lord decided to create the beasts of the field and the additional fowls of the air. It was also indicated that the Lord formed these beasts of the field from the "ground." Was this the "ground" of the earth, or the "ground" of Eden?

*Genesis 2:15-19: 15And the LORD God took the man and **put** him into the Garden of Eden to dress it and to keep it. 16And the LORD God commanded the man, saying, of every tree of the garden you may freely* *eat:* *¹⁷But of the tree of the knowledge of good and evil, you shalt not eat of it: for in the day that you eat thereof you shalt surely die. ¹⁸And the LORD God said, it is not good that the man should be alone; I will make him a help meet for him. ¹⁹And **out of the ground** the LORD God formed every beast of the field, and every fowl of the air; and brought them unto Adam to see what he would call them: and whatsoever Adam called every living creature that was the name thereof.*

We see above that while Adam was in the garden that the Lord formed yet further "out of the ground." Yet, what "ground" is this? Is this ground of Genesis 2:19 the ground of the "earth," as indicated in the Septuagint? Is this "ground" a spiritual ground of Eden (third heaven)? In Genesis 2:7, Adam was formed from the "ground." This "ground" we know also has "dust." "And the Lord God formed man of the **dust of the ground** ...."

In Genesis 2:8 we also read that the Lord planted a garden in Eden; and in Genesis 2:9, a continuation of Genesis 2:8, we see that "out of the **ground** made the Lord to grow every tree that is pleasant to the sight and good for food; the **tree of life** also in the midst of the **garden** ...." Is this "ground" the same "ground" that Adam was formed out of? Or is this the "ground" of Eden, the third heaven?

Genesis 2:7-9: *⁷And the LORD God formed man of the dust of the **ground and** breathed into his nostrils the breath of life; and man became a living soul. ⁸And the LORD **God planted a garden eastward in Eden; and there** he **put** the man whom he had formed. ⁹And out of the ground made the LORD God to grow every tree that is pleasant to the sight, and good for food, **the tree of life** also in the midst of the garden, and the tree of knowledge of good and evil.*

The fact that the Lord planted a garden in Eden shows that there had to be some kind of "ground" in which these trees were planted. Genesis 2:9 also stated that the tree of life was in the middle of this garden that the Lord planted in Eden; and that "out of the ground made the Lord God grow every tree." We have learned from Revelation 2:7 coupled with 2 Corinthians 12: 2-4 that "Paradise" is the "third heaven" where the "tree of life still exists. Genesis said that the tree of life is in the garden in Eden. Therefore, as indicated previously, "Eden" is "Paradise" (Genesis 2:8-9 with Revelation 2:7). "Paradise" is "third heaven according to Paul in 2 Corinthians 12:2-4. It follows that there must be "ground" in the third heaven in which trees can grow.

If one also read Genesis 2, Genesis 3, and parts of Genesis 4, it will also become clear that Eden (third heaven) was so intertwined with the earth that it is difficult to distinguish them. In Genesis 2 we learn that a river went out from Eden (third heaven) to water the garden in Eden. This same river then flowed to the earth to and parted into four rivers into countries like "Ethiopia" that we know still exists today; and the "river Euphrates" that still exists today.

In Genesis 4:16 we learn that Cain (after he murdered his brother) "dwelled in the land of Nod. on the east of Eden." Therefore, we can infer that Eden was still visible or perceivable though not accessible due to God's action in Genesis 2:24. With that said, there is an earth that can be seen with our nature eyes (we see it every day). Yet, the Lord Jesus indicates that there may be an earth that cannot be seen with the natural eyes.

*Matthew 12:40: For as Jonas was **three days and three nights** in the whale's belly; so, shall the Son of man be **three days and three nights** in the **heart of the earth.***

Jesus was "three days and three nights in the heart of the earth." We also learned from Paul that the "heart of the earth" is in reality "death" and the "abyss." We also learned in Acts that Hades is in the heart of the earth. There is a sphere in the earth that cannot be appreciated by our natural eyes.

*Romans 10:6-7: 6But the righteousness of faith speaks in this way, "Do not say in your heart, 'Who will ascend into heaven?'" (That is, to bring Christ down from above) 7or, "'who will descend into the **abyss?**'" (That is, to bring Christ up from the dead).*

When Jesus died, we all know that he descended into the abyss. Jesus labeled this "abyss" "as the heart of the earth." In Acts 2:31 we learn that Jesus was not "left in Hades." Therefore, "Hades" must also be in "the heart of the earth." The "abyss" and Hades is "in the heart of the earth." There is a spiritual dimension to the earth that we cannot necessarily see with our natural eyes. There is an invisible heavenly sphere on earth. Why is all this important to know? This is important to know relative to the question: "where did God make the serpent."

Thus, it has to be established that there is a "ground" in Eden (third heaven). It must also be understood that there is an invisible sphere of the earth as established by Jesus (the heart of earth is the place of the abyss and Hades). It must also be understood that prior to Adam's fall, the heaven and the earth were so entwined that it was difficult to tell them apart (the same heavenly water that watered the garden, also flowed to the four rives of the earth). Now let us discuss the "ground" from which "the serpent … 'part of' the beasts of the field" was made.

Genesis 2:15; 18: *[15]And the LORD God took the man and **put** him into the garden of Eden to dress it and to keep it …. [18]And the LORD God said, it is not good that the man should be alone; I will make him a help meet for him. [19]And **out of the ground** the LORD God formed every **beast of the field,** and every fowl of the air ….*

Genesis 2:18-19, LXX: *[18]And the Lord God said, it is not good that the man should be alone, let us make for him a help suitable to him. [19]**And God formed yet farther** out of the **earth** all the wild beasts of the field, and all the birds of the sky ….*

The Septuagint states that the Lord "formed **yet farther** out of the **earth** all the wild beasts of the field." The Hebrew text states that "out of the **ground** the Lord formed every beasts of the field …." If we follow the "text" of God's statement, we see that the man was in the garden at the time when God declared that he would make a "helpmeet" for Adam; therefore the "ground" that the beasts of the field (spiritual beasts of the field) were made from was the ground of the garden in Eden. If this "ground" was so intertwined with the earth, then they may have been made from the invisible ground of the earth. With that said, just as Paul in 2 Corinthians 12 could not tell if he was in the body or out of the body when he encountered the man who went to the third heaven, so likewise I cannot tell if the serpent, Satan, was made from the ground of the garden, outright, or the ground of "earth" (invisible sphere) as defined by the Septuagint in Genesis 2:18.

Based on the context of Genesis 2:8-9 and Genesis 2:15-19; it seems to me that the serpent was made from the ground of the garden in Eden, intertwined somehow with the "earth." This should not be strange that God created the serpent in Eden. In Ezekiel 28 we also learn that the Lord created additional "cherubs" in Eden. Now at one point in my life, I taught that this "cherub" in Ezekiel 28 could have been Satan and/or a "man." However, if we look at the text, this "cherub"[17] is indeed either a "man" or it is "the king of Tyre" — a cherub (not Satan) that covered the stones of fire.

As we will see later, the elders of other ages have erroneously named the serpent, "Lucifer;" they (we) have also inaccurately named him "king of Tyre." As we will see in subsequent chapter, if we stay in the context of Isaiah 14, we will see that "Lucifer" is in reality the "king of Babylon."

Do we call the "kings of Persia in Daniel 10, Satan himself? The answer is no! Then, why should we call the "king of Babylon" Satan, himself? We should not! However, Heylel, the king of Babylon can indeed be termed as part of the corporate Satan, but not Satan himself. It follows that "the king of Tyre" is just that a spirit "king of Tyre" that rules over the "prince of Tyre."

Ezekiel 28:12-15: *[12]Son of man, take up a lamentation upon the **king of Tyrus**, and say unto him, thus says the Lord GOD; you seal up the sum, full of wisdom, and perfect in beauty. [13]You **have been in Eden** the garden of God; every precious stone was thy covering, the sardius, topaz, and the diamond, the beryl, the onyx, and the jasper, the sapphire, the emerald, and the carbuncle, and gold; the workmanship of thy tabrets and of thy pipes was prepared in you in the day that you were created. [14]You are **the anointed cherub** that covers; and I have set you so; you were*

---

[17] Cherubs do also provide spiritual truth concerning those redeemed by the blood of the Lamb of God and the two witnesses in Revelation 11. You may refer to some of my other books for additional information on this topic (i.e., *The Numbers of God; Jesus' Resurrection, Our Inheritance; The Time Came, etc.*

upon the holy mountain of God; you have walked up and down in the midst of the stones of fire. ¹⁵You was perfect in thy ways from the day that you were created, till iniquity was found in thee.

The Scripture reference above shows that the king of Tyre "'existed' in **Eden**, the garden of God...." This same king is also called an "anointed cherub." Thus, one must conclude that in Ezekiel's mind, his understanding of the "anointed cherub" had to be relative to the cherubs he already saw as documented in Ezekiel 1 and Ezekiel 10 of his book. Ezekiel saw huge living creatures, with man's form, and four faces which he called cherubs — spiritual living creatures. Attention must also be given to the words **"has been"** ("hayah") in verse thirteen relative to the king of Tyre being in Eden the Garden of God. For this, I will cite the Septuagint (LXX).

The Septuagint (LXX) translates the Hebrew word "hayah" to the Greek word "egeneéthees" an inflection of "gennao" which is defined as, "was," **"was born,"** "to become," "came into being," "kin," "to generate," "procreate." This Greek word is also used in John 9:34 (New Testament), and Job 15:7 of the Old Testament (Septuagint).

John 9:34, NKJ: They answered and said to him, "You were completely born (lit., egenneéthees) in sins, and are you teaching us....

Ezekiel 28:13, Septuagint, (LXX): You was (lit., egeneéthees) in ... the paradise of God ....

Job 15:7a. Septuagint, (LXX): ... Art you the first man that was born (lit., egeneéthees) ...?

The Septuagint is saying that whoever, the "king of Tyre" is, he **"was"** in Eden the Garden of God; and he **"was born"** in Eden the Garden of God. The Scripture then called him an "anointed cherub." This makes this king of Tyre — the anointed cherub[18] — of another order, other than a natural king. Pointing to the time of the

---

[18] Note: As indicated previously, in certain context, cherubs point to the two witnesses in Revelation 11. Please refer to my books, *Jesus' Resurrection, Our Inheritance, The Time Came, The Last Hour, The First Hour, The Forty-second Generation, etc.*

first Adam, the anointed cherub was born or came into being in the Garden of Eden, after the first Adam. The Lord created these particular cherubs to help Adam. They are unique because they were created upon the earth in the Garden of Eden (heaven on earth).

The cherubim that Ezekiel saw in Ezekiel, Chapter One, have four faces each of a man, a lion, an ox, and an eagle. (The "face of a man" points to the Man Jesus who shed His Blood in the sweat of His "face" for us (Genesis 3:19a w/Luke 22:44). The face of the lion speaks of Jesus' as the "Lion of the tribe of Judah" who has "prevailed to open the scroll and to lose its seven seals" (Revelation 5:5; Joshua 15:14-19; etc.)

The "face of an ox" indicates Jesus as the "traveler" who traveled from heaven to earth to be a peace offering for us (John 3:13 w/Romans 5:1, Colossians 3:15, etc.). The eagle testifies of Jesus' heavenly dimensions (i.e., Jesus' heavenly origin, Jesus' heavenly perspective, Jesus' heavenly ascension, and so on (see the book of John).

In Genesis 2:18-19, one of the living creatures of the field were defined by Adam as a "serpent 'a part of' the beasts of the field" The serpent is a cherub (angel) with four faces (serpent, dragon, Devil, Satan); and like the "king of Tyre," the serpent was also made in the Garden of Eden. Again, to reiterate, this makes the serpent a junior to mankind in general; yet he was made before Mrs. Adam (Eve), but not "created" before Eve.

Thus, we now see the answer to the question: where did God make the serpent? The serpent was made in the garden after the man Adam. Therefore, relatively speaking the serpent is a "novice" with respect to the man Adam. Mankind in general (because we were in Adam's loin) is senior to the serpent and the corporate Satan! Jesus reestablished this seniority over serpents and scorpion beasts when he gave us "authority to tread on serpents and scorpions, and over all the powers of the enemy; and **nothing** shall by any means hurt you" (Luke 10: 19; Revelation 9:3-4).

The Novice

1 Timothy 3:1; 6: ¹*This is a true saying, if a man desires the office of a* **bishop,** *he desires a good work ....* ⁶*Not a* **novice,** *lest being lifted up with pride he falls into the* **condemnation** *of the devil.*

I have been saying throughout this book that the tempter was made after Adam, which makes the serpent a junior to Adam or a novice to Adam. The spirits of Mr. Adam and Mrs. Adam were "created" before "that 'original' serpent, called the Devil and Satan." However, God formed the male Adam, before he formed the female Adam. That is there is a difference between "creating" (Hebrew "bara" — to create out of nothing); in comparison with, "make" (Hebrew "asha" — to make out of something).

It seems to me that Mr. and Mrs. Adam spirits were both "created" before the Lord formed a body for them. It is clear from Genesis 2 that the Lord "built" the woman **after** he formed the man. This is one of the reasons why Paul declared that a wife is not to "usurp authority over the man ... for Adam was **first formed,** then Eve" (1 Timothy 1:12-13). It is also clear in Genesis 2 that the "original serpent" is formed after Adam. Therefore, the serpent cannot usurp authority over the man (the Man Jesus or any man that is in Christ). The serpent is junior to humans. The serpent is a novice to Adam; and consequently, the serpent is a novice relative to all humans because were in Adam's loins.

Hebrews 7:9-10: And as I may so say, Levi also, who receives tithes, paid tithes in Abraham. For he was yet in the loins of his father when Melchizedek met him.

As can been seen in the verse above, Levi participated in the action of his forefather Abraham because he was in the loins of his forefather via the "seed" that would eventually produce Isaac, from Isaac came Jacob and from Jacob came Levi. Thus, all the seed of Abraham participated in Abraham action because they were in his loins. The same is true for our seniority over the serpent. We are senior to the serpent because we also were in the loins of Adam when the Lord created and made him. Hence, the Devil is a novice to all mankind through Adam being the first man to be created, which was before the serpent was made.

*1 Timothy 3:1; 6: ¹This is a true saying, if a man desires the office of a **bishop**, he desires a good work …. ⁶Not a **novice**, lest being lifted up with pride he falls into the **condemnation** of the devil.*

In the reference above we see Paul's encouragement to those who desire the office of a bishop (lit., "overseer"). Paul continued his exhortation with a caution. He said that bishops should "not (be) a **novice** lest being lifted up with prided he fall into the **'crime'** of the devil." This verse is full of wisdom from the Lord Jesus. First, the Devil is compared to a "novice." Second, the word "condemnation" in verse six is transliterated as "crime" from the Greek word "krima." The Devil is also compared to a "bishop" (overseer). Here is an understanding.

In Revelation 12:7 we learn that the original serpent has angels that he oversees. The Scriptures reads: "the dragon fought and his angels;" and the Scriptures continued to say that "… the 'original' serpent … was cast out … and **his angels** with him" (Revelation 12:7; 9). Thus, it is apparent that the Devil has angels that he "oversees" who are called **"his angels."** With respect to the Devil being a "novice," I have shown repeatedly from Genesis 2 that the serpent, Satan, was made after Adam; and therefore, the serpent is a junior to Adam and a novice relative to Adam being "formed first."

The next item that Paul identified was "the crime of the Devil" that is related to Satan being a "novice" (newly planted). The Devil's crime was that he was/is "lifted up with pride." "Lifted up with pride," per definitions in Strong's Concordance dictionary, is also defined as: "to make a smoke," "to consume without flames," or he was "inflated with self-conceit." Thus, one of the serpent's early crimes was that he was "inflated with self-conceit" being a "novice," he lifted up himself over other beasts of the field. It appears to me this inflated self-conceit is related to the fact that the serpent did "not remain in the truth." That is, he left the truth of Jesus' command and inflated himself with his ego or narcissism.

Especially, after Adam rejected the devil's temptation by not selecting it as his helpmeet.

Genesis 2:15; 18-20; 3:1: *2:15And the LORD God took the man and put him into the garden of Eden to dress it and to keep it ....2:18 And the LORD God said, it is not good that the man should be alone; I will make him a help meet for him. 2:19And out of the ground the LORD God formed every* **beast of the field,** *and every fowl of the air; and brought them unto Adam* **to see what he would call them** *... 2:20And Adam gave names to all cattle, and to the fowl of the air, and to every beast of the field;* **but for Adam there was not found a help meet for him.** *3:1Now the serpent was 'subtle a part of all the'19 beast of the field which the LORD God had made ....*

The novice serpent was made as a test to Adam. The Lord made the first set of "helpmeets" **"to see"** what Adam would call them." Thus, they were originally made to "test" Adam **"to see"** if Adam would call them a help suitable for him. Adam rejected them as his "helpmeet." Adam passed the first test. That is, Adam also rejected bestiality! The fact that Adam rejecting the serpent from being called his helpmeet, I believe, is one of the reasons why the Devil fell into the "crime" of becoming inflated in self-ego. Jesus said that that the Devil "'remained not in the truth." Jesus also taught that the serpent speaks "from his own." Jesus is the truth! Therefore, sometime after the serpent was made, he decided **not** to remain in the truth of Jesus (i.e., Jesus' directions, commands, and so on). That is, he apparently decided to tempt beyond God's original limits.

John 8:44: You are of [your] father the devil, and the lusts of your father you will do. He was a murderer from the beginning, and **abode not in the truth,** *because there is no truth in him. When he speaks a lie, he speaks 'from' his own; for he is a liar, and the father of it.*

John 14:6: Jesus says unto him, **I am** *the way,* **the truth,** *and the life; no man comes unto the Father, but by me.*

---

[19] This literal rendition in the single quote was supplied by the authority for clarity.

Apparently, sometime after the Lord made the serpent, he also began to **"speak from his own"** self. Paul labeled this crime as being "inflated with self-conceit." According to the apostle Paul, the Devil's crime of self-conceit was due to the Devil being a novice relative to Adam. The serpent, a novice, **apparently made himself** overseer of the other beasts of the field; and may have tried to usurp "authority" (oversee) Mr. Adam of his own will after Mr. Adam rejected him as helpmeet.

When Adam rejected him as a helpmeet; and since the serpent's tests was overcome by Adam; the serpent must have decided from himself not to remain in the truth of Jesus and being a novice, he decided to lift himself above God's commands and some angels, now called "his angels." This pride eventually spilled over to Mrs. Adam after the Lord made her and Adam became "head over heels" about his new and only wife.

With all that said, it is clear that the apostle Paul also considered the Devil a novice. It is also clear from Paul teaching that the Devil's crime of self-conceitedness is link to the Devil being newly planted; or the Devil made himself an overseer. Paul's teaching in 1Timothy 3:1 coupled with 1 Timothy 3:6 demolishes this so called "gap theory" concerning the so-called catastrophe supposedly caused by the Devil in Genesis 1:1-2. The Devil was not even made then, according to the sequence in Genesis 2! So how could he have caused this so-called catastrophe in Genesis 1:2?

Some in the Church of Jesus give too much power to the Devil. The Devil is not stronger than Jesus; and therefore, the Devil is not stronger than us. The Devil is not wiser than "Jesus who is made unto us the wisdom of God;" and therefore the serpent is not wiser than us. Jesus created the serpent in the Garden after He Made man. Therefore, the Devil is also a novice to all mankind. We were and are commanded to bruise the serpent under our feet. "All things are subjected to Jesus!"

The Tempter

Genesis 2:19: *And out of the ground the LORD God formed every beast of the field, and every fowl of the air; and brought them unto Adam* **to see** *what he would call them: and whatsoever Adam called every living creature, which was the name thereof.*

1 Thessalonians 3:5: *For this cause, when I could no longer forbear, I sent to know your faith, lest by some means* **the tempter** *have tempted you, and our labor be in vain.*

Matthew 4:1; 3-4: *Then was Jesus led up of the Spirit into the wilderness to be* **tempted** *of the* **devil....** *³And when* **the tempter** *came to him, he said, if you be the Son of God, command that these stones be made bread. ⁴But he answered and said,* **it is written,** *Man shall not live by bread alone, but by every word that proceeds out of the mouth of God.*

The Lord made the serpent to be a tempter. Matthew defined "the tempter" as the devil. That was always the nature of the serpent — a tempter. The serpent did not fall to become a tempter as some teach; he was made a tempter. In the garden when the Lord continued to make further the beasts of the field, the serpent was a part of or from these beasts and fowls.

The Lord originally made them **"to see"** if Adam would call them a "helpmeet." Thus, they were made as "tempters" or "testers" from the beginning. The first time he encountered the Devil, Adam also called him a serpent, "a hisser or a whisperer of magic spells." Paul also called the Devil a "tempter." We also see that the Devil "tempted" Jesus just as the Devil tempted Adam in the Garden.

The question is: if the serpent was made a tempter why did the Lord curse him? This is a good question; and since most could not answer this question in some of the previous generations and ages, some of the elders have invented erroneous teachings. With that said, let us look at the Scriptures as to why the tempter was cursed in order to also show that the serpent was always a tempter.

Genesis 3:13-14: *¹³And the LORD God said unto the woman, what is this that you have done? And the woman said, the serpent* **beguiled** *me,* *and I did eat. ¹⁴And the LORD God said unto the serpent because you have **done this, you** are cursed above all cattle, and above every beast of the field; upon thy belly shalt you go, and dust shalt you eat all the days of thy life.*

The verses above are very telling. Mrs. Adam said that she ate from the tree that was off-limits because the serpent **"beguiled"** her. The Lord then responded to the serpent by saying "because you have **done this,** you are cursed above all ...." The Hebrew word for **"beguile"** also means to lend with interest, and to dun for payment on a debt. This tells us that this was not Mrs. Adam's first encounter with the serpent; and whatever their other encounters consist of, she now owed him payment for them. Somehow, she became indebted to the previous temptations of serpent. The serpent could now harass (dun) her for payment of some debt.

An interesting note at this point is that the Hebrew base word translated as "beguile" (NShA) means "to lend with interest," "to dun for payment" has a letter in it, "shin" (Sh), which is hieroglyphics of a **"tooth"** that pictorially also means to eats or to devour. Thus, she may have been tricked by him to believe that she had previously eaten something that was bad for her. If this was the case, he lied to her because the only tree that was forbidden to eat from was the tree of the knowledge of good and evil. The pictograph of the "tooth" may also mean that she was beguiled by the serpent because she was bitten[20] by him.

With that understood, the Lord then weighed in on the serpent by saying "because you have **done this,** you are cursed above all ...." The phrase "because you have done **this"** implies that the serpent did some other things that were not necessarily approved by the Father; and God may have overlooked them for a season.

However, when the serpent **"done this"** temptation of getting them (Mr. and Mrs. Adam) to eat from the tree of the knowledge of good and evil, the serpent had stepped into the area of going

---

[20] It is also worthy to note that the "mark" of the beast discussed in the book of Revelation is linked to being "bitten" by the beast. That is, when the Greek word "charagma" (mark) was first used by Sophocles, he used it of a serpent's bite.

beyond the commands of God. The New Testament calls this "covetousness" or "desiring the larger portion." The serpent was apparently not content with the angels he already oversees.

He was also not content to be subjected to the Adams. The serpent became too prideful to remain a junior (novice) to the Adams. Thus, he desired the larger part and overstepped his allotted limits of temptation. Even more importantly, the serpent was also not content to "abide in the truth" — Jesus; and therefore, overreached beyond the truth to father the lie (John 8:44). The lie in this case is that the serpent began to "speak from himself" and left the truth of God's commands.

*2 Corinthians 2:11: Lest **Satan should get an advantage** of us: for we are not ignorant of his devices.*

The phrase "should get an advantage" literally means "holding (desiring) more," "eager for gain," "to overreach," and "covetous" (Strong's NT #4122 and #4123). Therefore, Satan tends to "overreach;" he is "eager for gain;" he "desires more" than he supposed to have. Satan wants "an advantage." In his zeal, he overreached by appointing himself overseer of some angels that are now "his angels." The serpent also "coveted" the things God gave to Mr. and Mrs. Adam. This should make it a little simpler as to why he overreached in his temptation of Mrs. Adam. This should also show why God cursed the serpent.

The serpent was not cursed to become a tempter. On the contrary, the serpent was cursed for going too far with its temptation as a tempter. He was indeed made to be a tester; however, he overreached in his temptation. He tricked Mrs. Adam and dunned her for a payment of a debt owed; and thus, the tempter tempted her to go beyond God's command. She fulfilled the "covetousness" of the serpent. That is, she also "coveted" the tree that was placed off-limits by God.

"And when the woman saw that the tree was good for food, and that it was pleasant to the eyes, and a tree to be **desired (or coveted)** to make one wise, she took of the fruit thereof, and did eat, and gave also unto her husband with her; and he did eat" **(Genesis 3:6).** Jesus was opposite Mr. and Mrs. Adam. The temptation of the Devil had no effect on or in Jesus. Jesus overcame the Devil by using the Word of God. Jesus did what Mr. and Mrs. Adam should have done.

Matthew 4:1-11: *[1]Then was **Jesus** led up of the Spirit into the wilderness to be **tempted** of the devil. [2]And when he had fasted forty days and forty nights, he was afterward hungry. [3]And when **the tempter** came to him, he said, if you be the Son of God, command that these stones be made bread. [4]But he answered and said, **it is written**, man shall not live by bread alone, but by every word that proceeds out of the mouth of God. [5]Then the Devil taketh him up into the holy city, and sets him on a pinnacle of the temple, [6]and says unto him, if you be the Son of God, cast thyself down: for it is written, He shall give his angels charge concerning thee: and in their hands they shall bear you up, lest at any time you dash thy foot against a stone. [7]**Jesus said unto him, it is written again,** you shalt not tempt the Lord thy God. [8]Again, the Devil taketh him up into an exceeding high mountain, and shows him all the kingdoms of the world, and the glory of them; [9]And says unto him, all these things will I give thee, if you wilt fall down and worship me. [10]**Then says Jesus unto him,** get you hence, Satan: **for it is written,** you shalt worship the Lord thy God, and him only shalt you serve. [11]Then the Devil leaves him, and behold, angels came and ministered unto him.*

Jesus did what Mr. and Mrs. Adam should have done. They should have said "the LORD God commanded [us] … of the tree of the knowledge of good and evil, we shall **not** eat of it" (Genesis 2:16-17). We are to do the same. We are to use the Scripture to overcome the tempter. Let us be like Jesus and use the Word of God to overcome. **"The Word is near you, even in your mouth and in your heart, the Word of faith which we preach"** (Romans 10:8). We must learn to speak with the Lord's Words!

Who Named Satan, Lucifer?

*Isaiah 14:12, KJV: How are you fallen from heaven, **O Lucifer (heylel),** son of the morning! How are you cut down to the ground, which didst weaken the nations!*

The name "Lucifer" as translated in the King James Version was not used by Jews or early Christians as a name for Satan. Men by the name of "Origen" (185-254), "Tertullian" (155-220), and then "Jerome," in the latter part of the 4th century were among the first to translate the Hebrew word "Heylel" to Lucifer. Lucifer is not the proper name for Satan, but a Latin translation for "day star" used to translate "heylel."

With that said, the context of Isaiah 14 is regarding the "king of Babylon." Isaiah stated that "the people" would "take up this proverb against the **king of Babylon,** and say, how has the oppressor ceased! The golden city ceased" (Isaiah 14:4)! Isaiah continued his "proverb" in Isaiah 14:12 saying, "How are you fallen from heaven, O **'heylel,'** son of the morning! How are you cut down to the ground, which didst weaken the nations!"

Isaiah 14:12 is a continuation of the conversation that began in Isaiah 13:1; "The burden of **Babylon,** which Isaiah the son of Amoz did see;" which continued in Isaiah 14:4 saying that the people shall "take up this proverb against the **king of Babylon,** and say, how has the oppressor ceased, the golden city ceased." If Lucifer is indeed an invisible angel, then this angel is the spirit "king of Babylon." This, king's name is "Heylel." Lucifer is not the name for Heylel or the name for the Devil!

There is indeed an invisible "prince of Persia" and many invisible "kings of Persia." Gabriel, one of the arch angels, made this truth known to Daniel when Gabriel and Michael, one of the other chief princes, encountered them in the heavens (Daniel 10:13). There is also a "prince of Greece" that both Gabriel and Michael, the arch angels had to bind. (Daniel 10:20). Jeremiah 51:11, states that there is "the **spirit of** the kings of the Medes."

"In the first of Darius the Mede," Gabriel stood with Michael to "bind" the king of Babylon in order that the "spirit of the kings of the Medes" may rule (Jeremiah 51:11 w/Daniel 11:1). These verses prove that there is a spirit behind every kingdom or government in the earth. In fact, God calls most government systems "beasts;" and the leopard beast in Revelation 13 was given its authority by Satan (compare Daniel 7; Revelation 13; Revelation 17). The spirit behind Babylon is king "heylel." Lucifer is not the name of Satan or Satan himself.

Satan is indeed called many names, but Lucifer is not one of them. Heylel is the name used of the "king of Babylon." It does not appear that Jerome intended to make Lucifer a proper name, because in 2 Peter 1:19 "day star" is also translated as "Lucifer" in Jerome's Latin translation. Who is this "day star" in 2 Peter 1:19, translated to read "Lucifer" by Jerome? The "Day-Star" in 2 Peter 1:19 is certainly not refereeing to Satan! The "Day-Star" in 2 Peter 1:19 is referring to the "sure prophetic Word" and/or Jesus, the Christ, the Son of the living God. Certainly, Jerome did not call the Word of God, "Lucifer" in context of how the word have morphed to mean "Satan." On the contrary, he merely was translating a Greek word "phosphorous" as close as he could to Latin.

*2 Peter 1:19: We have also a **more sure word of prophecy;** whereunto you do well that you take heed, as unto a light that shines in a dark place, until the day dawn, and the **Day Star (lit., light-bearer ("phosphorous"))** arise in your hearts.*

We know the "Day Star" to be the "sure prophetic Word" of God and/or Jesus. Thus, when Jerome translated this Greek word "phosphorous" in Latin as "Lucifer," he certainly was not calling God's Word "Lucifer" in the sense as "Lucifer" has come to mean. It is also worthy to note that the Septuagint (LXX) translated the Hebrew word "heylel" as "phosphorous" **not** "Lucifer." And I must also say that Jesus, Paul, Peter, John, James, and so on all used and quoted the Septuagint (LXX). If, "heylel" in Isaiah 14:12 was referring to Satan, I am quite sure the translators of the Hebrew Bible to Greek would have translated it as "satanas" (the Greek word for Satan).

For example, Psalms 40:6 translated from the Hebrew version reads: *"Sacrifice and offering you did not desire; **mine ears have you opened**: burnt offering and sin offering have you not required."* Here are how the translators of the Septuagint translated Psalms 40:6: *"Sacrifice and offering you would not; **but a body have you prepared me**: whole-burnt-offering and [sacrifice] for sin you did not require."* Yes, you read that last quote correctly.

The translator translated the phrase **"mine ears have you opened"** to **"a body you have prepared me."** This same Septuagint translation of Psalms 40:6 was quoted by the writer of the Book of Hebrew in Hebrews 10:5. There are other examples of this practice of the translators of the Hebrew Bible to the Greek Septuagint as verified by Jesus.

That is, Jesus also quoted the Septuagint. The Hebrew phrase translated as **"ordained strength"** in Psalms 8:2 is translated in the Septuagint as **"perfected praised"** in Matthew 21:16, as stated by Jesus. There are other examples of this in the Septuagint. Thus, it is apparent to me that if the Jews wanted to translate "heylel" as Satan, they could have. However, they **did not** translate "heylel" as "satanas."

With that said, I concluded with this, Jerome used this word ("Lucifer") in his Latin Vulgate in Isaiah 14:12, Job 11:17, Job 38:32, and 2 Peter 1:19. It appears that the traditions of men have made this word ("Lucifer") a proper name for Satan. There is no basis for this in the Scriptures (Greek or Hebrew versions).

Worshipper, "Worder," Warrior

Some of the traditional teachings of men have also invented the idea that Satan was among three main angels. They have called Michael, the arch angel, the "warrior" angel. They have called Gabriel, the "worder" angel; that is, Gabriel delivers words from God to the believers. They have labeled Satan as the "worshipper" angel. This sound catchy—"worshipper," "worder," and "warrior." However, is this labeling and doctrine healthy, even though some of these titles manifest in the angels among other manifestations? Let us look at the Scriptures and see.

There are indeed seven angels[21] that stand before God, according to Revelation 8:2. There are also seven angels (men) of the Church, according to Revelation 1:20. In this book, I will look at the seven arch angels, who are also a part of the "elect angels" (1 Timothy 5:21). According to the **Talmud, they are** *Michael, Gabriel, Raphael, and Uriel;* and according to **1 Enoch 20**, there is *Michael, Gabriel, Raphael, Uriel, Raguel, Saraqâêl, and Remiel.*

Here are the meanings of their names. Michael, "he who is like God;" Gabriel, "mighty-man of God;" Raphael, "healer of God;" Uriel, "fire of God;" Raguel, "shepherd or friend of God;" Saraqâêl, "command of God;" and Remiel, "thunder of God." Michael, the archangel is found in the book of **Daniel, Jude,** and **Revelation.** Gabriel is found in **Daniel** and **Luke.** Raphael is found in the Apocryphal books in the book of **Tobit 12:15.** Michael is indeed called an "archangel" or "one of the chief angels."

Daniel 10:12-13: *[12]Then said he unto me, Fear not, Daniel: for from the first day that you didst set thine heart to understand, and to chasten thyself before thy God, thy words were heard, and I am come for thy words. [13]But the* **prince of the kingdom of Persia** *withstood me one and twenty days: but, lo,* **Michael, one of the chief princes,** *came to help me; and I remained there with the kings of Persia.*

---

[21] Please refer to my book, *The Days of the 7th Angel* for further understanding

*Jude 1:9: Yet **Michael** the **archangel,** when contending with the Devil he disputed about the body of Moses, durst not bring against him a railing accusation, but said, The Lord rebuke thee.*

We see in the references above that Michael is indeed one of the chief angels. In the New Testament, "chief" is translated to be "arch." Michael does indeed appear on the scene when there is resistance from other principalities. When the angel[22] in Daniel 10 were being withstood by the principality that ruled Persia, Michael came to assist in the fight; and Michal was able break this angel loose from the struggle with the invisible "prince (lit., chief) of Persia."[23] Does Michael, the arch angels fight? Absolutely, Yes! Yet does this give us the right to make him only a "warrior angel," as some has?

Michael's name means "who is like God." Do we really know what God is like? Can we, in our finite minds, define who God is? Is God only a warrior, as some have labeled Michael to be a "warrior angel?" Has God proclaimed His name to you?

*Exodus 34:6-8: [6]And the LORD passed by before him, and proclaimed, The LORD, The LORD God, **merciful** and **gracious, longsuffering,** and **abundant in goodness** and **truth,** [7]**keeping mercy** for thousands, **forgiving iniquity and transgression and sin,** and that will by no means clear the guilty; visiting the iniquity of the fathers upon the children, and upon the children's children, unto the third and to the fourth generation. [8]And Moses made haste, and bowed his head toward the earth, and **worshipped.***

Based on the Scriptures above, it does not appear to me that God's name or nature can be described as a "warrior." Only God can define Himself. It follows that Michael, the archangel, "who is like God" cannot be defined with one word. In addition, if the other

---

[22] This angel in Daniel 10 is presumed to be Gabriel that had previous interactions with Daniel.

[23] If we are to be consistent in our interpretation concerning Michael, an arch angel, being called "one of the chief princes," then "the prince of Persia" is also an "arch" or chief angels. However, the chief prince of Persia has become a resistance against the archangels Michael and Gabriel.

angel in Daniel 10 that Michael helped is indeed Gabriel, an archangel; Gabriel also engaged in the fight.

Daniel 10:20-21: *20Then said he, know you wherefore I come unto you? And now will I return to **fight** with the prince of Persia: and when I am gone forth, lo, the prince of Greece shall come. 21But I will show you that which is noted in the scripture of truth: and there is none that holds with me in these things, but **Michael your prince.***

The other angel together with Michael in Daniel 10 was also engaged in the "fight" against the prince of Persia. And if this other angel is indeed Gabriel, then, the so called "worder" angel is also a "warrior angel." The point is this, who gives mankind authority to determine that there are (were) three main angels relegated to certain duties? Who gives mankind authority to say that Satan was the main worshipper angel?

Who gave mankind the right to make Gabriel a "worder" angel? Including the Talmud and 1 Enoch, and using only the Bible that we have today, Gabriel is presumed to also be an archangel. With that said, I do believe that Gabriel is an arch angel. However, his name means "mighty man of God;" "warrior of God;" or "strong man of God." If anyone of the archangels' name relegates them to a "warrior" it must include Gabriel. Yet we know that Gabriel not only fights, but he also does indeed deliver messages.

With that said, Satan was created as a serpent. Yet some have labeled him as "chief worshipper." The four seraphs that were created to worship God are still worshipping God day and night according to Revelation 4 and Isaiah 6. Satan's fall is not that he fell from being a worshipper. Satan's fall was that He did not "remain" in the "truth" of Jesus; thus, Satan became a "man-faced-slayer" – Satan caused the death of the Adams in the garden and the death of Jesus on the cross.

Satan's fall was also result of what he caused Mr. and Mrs. Adam to do against God's commands. His fall was that he overreached his authority to cause the Adams to sin. Satan was always a tempter, he was made a serpent, and he is that original serpent identified in Revelation 12 and 2 Corinthians 11. Satan just overreached his authority as a tempter to become a usurper over mankind and apparently over some angels. This overreach was a direct result of Adam rejecting him as a helpmeet when Adan chooses Eve instead. In light of this let us look at some of the Scriptures that men have used to make Satan a so-called worshipper who eventually fell.

Isaiah 14:12-14: *12How are you fallen from heaven, O **Lucifer,** son of the morning! How are you cut down to the ground, which didst weaken the nations! 13For you have said in thine heart, I will ascend into heaven. I will exalt my throne above the stars of God: I will sit also upon the mount of the congregation, in **the sides of the north:** 14I will ascend above the heights of the clouds; I will be like the most High.*

As indicated in my previous chapter, Lucifer was not originally used as a proper noun. Lucifer is a Latin word used by Jerome to translate some Hebrew words and Greek words in Isaiah 14:12, Job 11:17, Job 38:32, and 2 Peter 1:19. The Hebrew word for "Heylel" is also translated as "howl" in the Scriptures; and the root word ("halal") from where heylel is derived is translated in the King James as "praise" 117 times, "glory" 14 times, "boast" 10 times, mad 8 times, shine 3 times, foolish 3 times, fools 2 times, "commended" 2 times, "rage" 2 times, "celebrate" 1 time, "give" 1 time, "marriage" 1 time, and "renowned" 1 time.

Zechariah 11:2: Howl, fir tree; for the cedar is fallen; because the mighty are spoiled: howl, O you oaks of Bashan; for the forest of the vintage is come down.

The word translated "howl" in the verse above is the same exact Hebrew word translated "Lucifer" by Jerome. Just this fact alone should let you know that we must be careful in how words are translated and used to mean something that may not convey the correct understanding. One of my teachers stated that if you want to know what is in a book, simply ask the author. In this case the author of the Bible is the Spirit of Jesus Christ.

So, would it read right to say "'**Lucifer'** fir tree; for the cedar is fallen ...." The answer is no! Or what if I translated Isaiah 14:12 as:

"how are you falls from heaven, O **'Howl,'** son of the morning …."
The answer is maybe not!

With that said, and as indicated above, the root word for "heylel" is also translated as "praise" one hundred and seventeen (117) in the King James. Thus, men have assumed that this so called "Lucifer" must have been "Satan" the worshipper ("one who praises"). If indeed "Heylel" is a worshipper, then this worshipper is the "king of Babylon," not Satan. In fact, if "praise" is meant to be understood, by Heylel, it appears to me that "praise" is what was lavished on this king of Babylon, not that he was necessarily a worshipper. Hear a couple of Scriptures concerning Babylon.

Jeremiah 51:41-42: *⁴¹How is **Sheshach** taken! And how is **the praise of the whole earth** surprised! How Babylon is become an astonishment among **the** nations! ⁴²The Sea is come up upon **Babylon:** she is covered with the multitude of the waves thereof.*

Isaiah 13:19: *And Babylon, the **glory of kingdoms,** the **beauty** of the Chaldees' excellency, shall be as when God overthrew Sodom and Gomorrah.*

If one studies Revelation 18 carefully, one will see that mystery Babylon is also praised by the masses. You would read phrases like "what city is like unto this great city!" So, Babylon was praised, and not necessarily one who "praises." In addition to this understanding, we read in Isaiah 14:13 that "Heylel" wanted to "sit upon the mount of the congregation, **in the sides of the north."** **"The sides of the north"** is where **"Mount Zion"** is located **"the city of the Great King"** (Psalm 48).

At the time when Isaiah 14 was written, the "mount of the congregation" is a name for the congregation of Israel. Today, the "mount of the congregation" is the Church, which resides in the spiritual "Zion" (1 Peter 2:4-6, Hebrew 12:22). Remember that "God," yes "God" raised up the natural king of Babylon to judge Israel by war and captivity (see Jeremiah, Ezekiel, Isaiah, etc.).

However, the king of Babylon and subsequent kings of Babylon wanted to exalt themselves even more over God's congregation and Mount Zion beyond God's original intent (Isaiah 14:4-6; Jeremiah 50:17-18; Daniel 5). With that said, Isaiah 14, a continuation of Isaiah 13, is about the judgment on Babylon and its king for Babylon's abuse against Israel.[24] Heylel is the "proverb" (lit. "pithy maxim," "simile") name for the king of Babylon.

Isaiah 14:4; 12-14: ³And it shall come to pass in the day that the LORD shall give you rest from thy sorrow, and from your fear, and from the hard bondage wherein you were made to serve, ⁴That you shall take up this **proverb** *against the* **king of Babylon,** *and say, how has the oppressor ceased! The golden city ceased! …. ¹²How are you fallen from heaven, O* **Lucifer,** *son of the morning! How are you cut down to the ground, which didst weaken the nations! ¹³For you have said in thine heart, I will ascend into heaven. I will exalt my throne above the stars of God: I will sit also upon the mount of the congregation, in* **the sides of the north:** *¹⁴I will ascend above the heights of the clouds; I will be like the most High.*

The scriptures above are clear. The "proverb" (simile) of the words in Isaiah 14:3-14 is concerning the "king of Babylon." And if the words point to an invisible king, then that invisible king is also the spirit over (Mystery) Babylon; the mystery Babylon that was revealed in Revelation 17. The other Scripture that men have used to teach that Satan was a worshipper is found in Ezekiel 28:13.

Again, I must also say that I once taught the same thing from Ezekiel 28 as the elders taught me until the Lord Jesus showed me the truth; even though there are principles in Ezekiel 28 that can be applied to Satan himself. With that said, we see in Ezekiel, the "king of Tyre" or the "king of Tyrus" is said to "seal up the **sum (lit., pattern)**; full of wisdom; perfect in beauty; he had "tabrets" (or drums, or tumbrels) and "pipes" prepared in him. From the fact that the king of Tyre had drums and pipes, the doctrine that Satan was a worshipper was developed.

Ezekiel 28:13: You have been in Eden the garden of God; every precious stone was thy covering, the sardius, topaz, and the diamond, the beryl, the onyx, and the jasper, the sapphire, the emerald, and the carbuncle, and

---

[24] This same abuse will once again happen against the saints of Jesus (the Israel of God) as shown in Revelation 17:5-6, and so on.

gold: *the workmanship of thy* **tabrets** *and of thy* **pipes** *was prepared in you in the day that you were created.*

Ezekiel 28:13*, NKJ: You were in Eden, the garden of God; every precious stone was your covering: The sardius, topaz, and diamond, Beryl, onyx, and jasper, Sapphire, turquoise, and emerald with gold. The workmanship of your* **timbrels** *and* **pipes** *was prepared for you on the day you were created.*

We have already discussed the king of Tyre in a previous chapter; and have established that this "king" is indeed a cherub that was created in Eden. We also established the truth that the of king Tyre is just that the king of Tyre (a part of the corporate Satan), not Satan, himself. The New Testament has clarified all the names of Satan. In Revelation 12, he called "the great dragon" "that 'original' serpent," Satan, Devil. In 1 John, he is also called "the wicked." In Thessalonians, he is called the "tempter."

In Matthew 12, Jesus and the Pharisees called Satan "Beelzebul"[25] (prince of the house). Paul called Satan a "tempter" which Matthew, Mark, and Luke indicated the same. In the Old Testament Satan is identified as "serpent," "Satan," "Leviathan," and the many "Baals." I have not found where Satan is called the king of Tyre or king Heylel. The king of Tyre was a "pattern" cherub; he was full of wisdom which he perverted to merchandising; complete in beauty; he was an anointed cherub that covered; he was set upon the holy mountain of God; and he walked in the middle of the stones of fire.

Ezekiel 28:14*: You are the anointed cherub that* **covers;** *and I have set you so: you were* **upon the holy mountain of God;** *you have walked up and down in the midst of the* **stones of fire.**

The Holy Mountain of God is defined in the Scriptures as the Lord's House (the Church), Jerusalem, Israel, and the mount of transfiguration (Isaiah 27:13; 66:20; Ezekiel 20:40; Daniel 9:16; 1 Peter 1:18). With that said, the Holy Mountain of God is also related

---

[25] Beelzebul means the master of the dung (feces); however, some follow Jerome's translation of "Beelzebub"—prince of the dung, or flies.

to the third heavens being understood in Jesus ascending far above the heavens. The "stones of fire" seems to be the precious stones that he covered and the precious stones that were on him in the bezels God had prepared in him.

*Isaiah 2:2: And it shall come to pass in the last days, that **the mountain of the LORD'S house** shall be established in the top of the mountains and shall be exalted above the hills; and all nations shall flow unto it.*

*Isaiah 27:13: And it shall come to pass in that day, that the great trumpet shall be blown, and they shall come ... and shall worship the LORD in **the holy mount at Jerusalem.***

*Ezekiel 20:40: For in mine **Holy Mountain** ... the height **of Israel** ....*

*2 Peter 1:18: And this voice which came from heaven we heard, when we were with him in the **holy mount.***

Therefore, the cherub, called the king of Tyre was somehow involved with the mountain of God. It appears that this cherub also covered with precious stones and was able to walk in the middle of these stones of fire. This is seen in God's statement to this cherub after the cherub sinned. "I will destroy thee, O **covering** cherub, from the midst **of** the **stones of fire**" (Ezekiel 28:16).

Maybe these stones of fire that he covered are the very precious stones that this cherub was himself covered with. In Job 28:5-6, precious stones in the earth (like sapphire) are related to "fire" beneath. According to the Scriptures, the "angelic ministry"[26] ("workmanship") of the "king of Tyre is that there was indeed in him the beauty of playing the tambourine or drums; and he also had "bezels" for the precious stones he was apparently covered with.

That is, this cherub was indeed involved with the playing of tambourines and drums, a form of worship and praise. He was also involved in the transporting of precious stones of fire, understood by the fact that he was "chamfered" for carrying precious stones

---

[26] In Ezekiel 28:13 "workmanship" (MLAKTh) is from the same Hebrew word for "angel" (MLAK)

that he eventually took as his own and merchandised them. Here is what the Holy Spirit by the Scriptures has taught me.

It appears to me by the Holy Spirit that the king of Tyre—the cherub—was an angel with the "pattern" and "wisdom" of how to cut precious stones to fit in a bezel or for New Jerusalem, the holy mountain of God. It is possible that the "beauty" of the cherub is the beauty he was to reproduce in the precious stones as he cut them for the bezels or for placement in New Jerusalem. He was also granted to "cover" (lit., fence, protect) these stones of fire. Instruments of music were "prepared in him" which was his "angelic duty;" and somehow, he began to "traffic" illegally which was his downfall. Isaiah 51:3 indicated that the "sound of melody (musical instruments)" is heard in the Garden of the Lord. Maybe this cherub was responsible for the music in the Eden.

*Isaiah 51:3: For the LORD shall comfort Zion: he will comfort all her waste places; and he will make her wilderness like Eden, and her desert like the **garden of the LORD**; joy and gladness shall be found therein, thanksgiving, and **the voice of melody.***

Remember, in addition to the "king of Tyre" being cast to the ground for merchandising his beauty and for corrupting his wisdom (Ezekiel 28:16-17). The Lord had also given him the beauty of wisdom to play the drums; he was given the beauty of wisdom as to how to cover (protect) the stones of fire; he was given the beauty of wisdom with regards to his "chamfer" that enabled him to transport these stones of fire. Eventually, he began to merchandise himself by merchandising the beauty of his wisdom, the ministry of his instruments, and the beauty of the precious stones that covered him.

It does not appear to me that Satan is indeed the worshipper discussed in Ezekiel 28 as some have affirmed. The cherub discussed in Ezekiel 28 is another cherub among the "living creatures" that were created in the Garden after Adam, but before Mrs. Adam. "That original serpent" is a great red dragon; not a head "worshipper." In fact, Satan was the opposite. The serpent is a usurper and was the first to father the concept of creature worship, instead of worshipping the Creator, because Adam chooses a woman for his wife <u>in lieu</u> of the beast of the field.

Satan's perversion of creature worshipping creature is the practice which eventually caused same sexuality. Nowhere in Ezekiel 28 is the king of Tyre, who is indeed a cherub, called a serpent, or a tempter, or Satan, or the Devil or a great dragon. The king of Tyre is just that the invisible king of Tyre, a cherub, that once ruled the kingdom of Tyre; just as the invisible prince of Greece ruled the kingdom of Greece; the invisible "kings of Persia" ruled the kingdom of Persia; and the "spirit of the Medes" ruled the kings of the Medes. The king of Tyre as per the description in Ezekiel 28 was not called "a tempter" or a "serpent." However, he has indeed become a part of the corporate Satan. Thus, he may now be called "Satan" in that sense.

Matthew 12:23-26: [23]*And all the people were amazed, and said, Is not this the son of David?* [24]*But when the Pharisees heard [it], they said, this [fellow] doth not cast out* **'demons,'** *but by* **Beelzebub the prince of the 'demons.'** [25]*And Jesus knew their thoughts, and said unto them, every kingdom divided against itself is brought to desolation; and every city or house divided against itself shall not stand:* [26]*And if* **Satan** *cast out* **Satan,** *he is divided against himself; how shall then his kingdom stand?*

In the verse above, we see that in the mind of the Pharisees, Beelzebub is the prince of demons. Jesus, then equated "Beelzebub" to "Satan" and he equated "demons" to a corporate "Satan." Note: as previously proved, "Satan," prince of demons, is different from "Satan," the demons. Thus, even though the king of Tyre is a "cherub" that fell; he is not Satan himself, but he is probably a part of the corporate Satan that was produced in the Garden, **after** Adam was created.

Man-Faced-Slayer

John 8:44: *You are of your father the devil, and the lusts of your father you will do. He was a* **murderer (lit., man-faced-slayer)** *from the* **beginning,** *and abode not in the truth, because there is no truth in him. When he speaks a lie, he speaks of his own: for he is a liar, and the father of it.*

One of the questions of the ages is why does it appears that the tempter and the principalities and powers have a "strong dislike" for anything "man-faced" (humans). We learn in John 8 that Satan was a "man-faced-slayer" ("murderer") from the beginning and that he did not abide in the truth.[27] We also know that Jesus is "the truth." Jesus is also "the Man"[28] that made the "man," Adam, and the "woman," Mrs. Adam who was taken out of Adam. We also learn in 1 John 3:15 that "hate," which literally means "a strong dislike," is equated to "murder" ("man-faced-slayer")

Thus, the Devil did not remain in the truth of Jesus, the Man; and the serpent became a hater of "the man Adam." That is, after Adam rejected the serpent as a help meet, the tempter did not abide in the truth of Jesus, "the Man;" and the serpent also hated Mrs. Adam, also known as "woman," apparently because Adam chose her (a "man-face" person) over him (a serpent faced cherub). The result of this "hate" was "murder" (slaying of the man-faced persons of Mr. and Mrs. Adam).

The Hebrew definition for Adam is "to show blood in the **face**" (see Strong's Concordance). The Hebrew hieroglyphics depiction of Adam is "strong-blood" or "first blood." When the Lord made the first set of help meet, He made them to "see" if Adam would indeed call them as "help meet." The word "help" means "to surround and protect." The word "meet" means "to stand in front of," or "to front."

Therefore, when Adam "saw" the beasts of the field and the fowls of the air the Bible said that he did not find any among them he

---

[27] John 8:44
[28] John 4:29

could call a help meet (Genesis 2:20). None of the beasts of the field and none of the fowls of the air were qualified to "front" Adam. Why? They did not look like him; they were not "man-faced." However, when Adam saw Mrs. Adam, his response was different! He like what he saw because she was human faced.

Genesis 2:21-23: *21And the LORD God caused a deep sleep to fall upon Adam, and he slept: and he took one of his ribs and closed up the flesh instead thereof; 22and the rib, which the LORD God had taken from man, made he a woman, and brought her unto the man. 23And Adam said, **this is now** bone of my bones, and flesh of my flesh: she shall be called **Woman,** because she was taken out of **Man.***

When the Lord built Mrs. Adam, he built here to be a "help meet," one who surrounds, protects, and stands in front of the man. When Mrs. Adam stood in front of Adam, he saw a human-faced person. Mrs. Adam is called "woman," which literally means "one who is taken out of man." Since she is from man, she is man-faced, and thus chosen by Adam to be his "help" to "front" him. Apparently when the serpent stood in front of Adam the first time, he saw a serpent-faced creature; hence Adam named him "serpent." With that said, we learn from Jesus that the prince of this world tends to listen in on conversation to get an advantage (John 4:30).

It appears to me that the serpent eavesdrops on Adam's conversation with the Lord, when Adam said, **"this one** is now bones of my bones and flesh of my flesh." That is, "this one," (Mrs. Adam) not serpents and not fowls; but "this one," Mrs. Adam is qualified to be called woman — she who comes from a man-faced person. The result of the acceptance of his wife and the rejection of the serpent has caused the serpent to hate women, marriages, and anything man-faced ever since. Here is why?

Man is made in the image of God. Jesus is the image of the invisible God.[29] Jesus is man-faced, "the Man." Jesus made Adam in his man-faced image. Mrs. Adam was taken out of Adam; and thus, she is also man-faced. The Devil did not remain in the truth of Jesus. That is, the Devil also did not abide in Jesus who is also "the

---

[29] Colossians 1:15

Man," or "the last Adam."[30] Because the Satan did not abide in the truth, which is Jesus, we can conclude that the serpent came to "hate" Jesus; thus, the serpent's "murder" (hate) of Jesus.

Or one can also conclude that the cause of Mr. and Mrs. Adam "death" is a result of the serpent hating Jesus, the Man. Adam was created in the image of God, which is the image of Jesus. Therefore, when the serpent tempted the Adams, and both Adams fell, that was a direct antagonist against God and Jesus, the man-faced Son of God. Let us look at some of the Scriptures that show this.

Genesis 1:26-27: [26]*And God said, let us make* **man in our image,** *after our likeness: and let them have dominion .... * [27]*So* **God created man in his own image, in the image of God created he him;** *male and female created he them.*

Colossians 1:13; 15: [13]*Who has delivered us ... into the kingdom of his dear* **Son** *.... * [15]**Who is the image of the invisible God,** *the firstborn of every creature.*

"The Son" — Jesus is "the image of the invisible God." Adam was created in the image of God; thus, Adam was created in the image of Jesus. The woman to whom Jesus ministered to at the well said to her village — "Come, see a **man**, which told me all things that ever I did: is not this **the Christ**" (John 4:29)? Jesus is also spoken of throughout the Scriptures as "the Son of **Man.**" The Devil was the first man-faced-slayer. That is, he hated Jesus, he did not abide in the truth; he also hated Mr. and Mrs. Adam. He murdered them with death. Why? One of the reasons is that they were "man-faced."

John 8:44: *You are of your father the Devil, and the lusts of your father you will do. He was a* **murderer (lit., man-faced-slayer)** *from the* **beginning,** *and abode not in the truth, because there is no truth in him. When he speaks a lie, he speaks of his own: for he is a liar, and the father of it.*

---

[30] 1 Corinthians 15:45

1 John 3:11-15: ¹¹*For this is the message that you heard from the beginning, that we should love one another.* ¹²*Not as Cain, who was **of that wicked one,** and slew his brother. And wherefore slew he him? Because his own works were evil, and his brother's righteous.* ¹³*Marvel not, my brethren, if the world hate you.* ¹⁴*We know that we have passed from death unto life because we love the brethren. He that loves not his brother abides in death.* ¹⁵*Whosoever **hates** his brother is a **murderer (lit., man-faced-slayer):** and you know that no murderer hath eternal life abiding in him.*

In John 8:44, Jesus said that the Devil is a murderer from the beginning. The Greek word used for "murderer" in John 8:44 is only used one other time in the Scripture, I John 3:15, quoted above. We see that this word "murder" — "man-faced-slayer" is equated to "hate" — "strong dislike." This word (murderer) is only used of Cain and the Devil. Cain was "of the wicked one" (the tempter); and thus, Cain was, in essence, "serpent-faced" in character. This concept is sound because Jesus and John, the Baptist called the Pharisees and Sadducees "'offspring' of serpents" (Matthew 3:7; 12:34; 23:33).

We know that Cain murdered Abel as the serpent caused the death of Mr. and Mrs. Adam. Abel is a type of Jesus who would be murdered by Cain as the Jews and Romans crucified Jesus. Abel in essence was "man-faced;" that is, Abel walked in the image of Jesus and was killed for it. The question is though: who did the Devil murder, or hate in order for Jesus to label him as a murderer?

The Devil hated Jesus and eventually became an accomplice in the murder of Jesus when it was the "hour" of "the authority of darkness" (Luke 22:53). The Devil hated and murdered Mr. and Mrs. Adam. The Lord said that Mr. and Mrs. Adam would "surely die" if they ate from the tree of the knowledge of good and evil. The Hebrew means that they would "die by death." We learn in Hebrews 2 that at one time the Devil had "the power of death."

Thus, when the serpent lied to Mrs. Adam, saying that she would not surely die if she ate from the tree that was off limits, which was his bate to slay, "by death," her and Adam. The Devil was the first to become a man-faced-slayer; and his first pupil (Cain) followed in his footstep. We also see that Mystery Babylon and the kingdom of Tyre became merchandisers of the "slaves (lit., bodies)" and the "souls of man-faced" (Revelation 18:13; Ezekiel 27:13). Why is this important to know?

We are not to hate; and we are not to murder. We are not to merchandise any souls, including any souls of man-faced humanity. It appears to me that the term "man-faced" is metaphor for those who manifest the human-face of Jesus. Thus, the "souls of man-faced" that were sold by the merchants of the earth to mystery Babylon can point to the Christians who were sold as slaves in the Roman Empire.

Any human who kills another human, is satanically motivated. Selling "man-faced" souls or the bodies of humans ("human trafficking") is wrong and satanically motivated. Paul said in 1 Corinthians 7:23b, "Do not be 'slaves' of men." Instead, we are to love one another as Jesus commanded. We are not to hate or have any strong dislike for our fellow man-faced brothers and sisters. "He that does not love his brother abides in death. Whosoever **hates** his brother is a **murderer (man-faced-slayer)** ...." (I John 3:14-15).

Let us love God with all our minds, soul, and strength; and let us love our neighbor as ourselves as Jesus has commanded us!

Jesus is Stronger than any Strong Man

For many years, I have had questions concerning Jesus' statement that He (Jesus) had bound the strong man (Satan), took his armor and spoiled Satan goods. I could not settle on what was this "armor" that Jesus took from the strong man. Finally, one day, my wife and I were discussing Revelation 12, when the Holy Spirit revealed to me what "armor" Jesus took from Satan. Jesus stripped the strong man of the armor of his strength. Yes, Satan is now weak. Jesus "a stronger than he" (Satan) has come upon Satan, "overcome him" and "took his armor."

Luke 11:20-22: *²⁰But if I with the finger of God cast out devils, no doubt the kingdom of God is come upon you. ²¹When a **strong man armed** keeps his palace, his goods are in peace: ²²But when a **stronger than he** shall come upon him, and overcome him, **he** taketh from him all his armor wherein **he** trusted and divides his spoils.*

The armor of the strong man was his strength; however, a stronger than he has come, and stripped Satan of his "armor" which was his strength. **Jesus, the "stronger than he,"** has overcome Satan and took his armor. "The strong man" was indeed "armed." The question must be asked, what was the strong man armed with?

He was "armed" with strength to tempt. However, Jesus weakened Satan by taking Satan's strength; and the Spirit of Jesus has been dividing his spoils by casting our demons. That is, Jesus took the strength of Satan away from Satan when Satan attempted to temp Jesus during the 40 days of trail in the wilderness. Jesus overcame Satan's temptation; and thus, Jesus' statement in the book of John that the former prince of this world (Satan) has nothing in Jesus.

That is, Satan is weak to Jesus, because Jesus overcame Satan' temptations in the 40 days wilderness trial. Thus, Satan is **"not strong enough"** to retain his goods—supplies that belong to mankind. Satan is not strong enough to withstand the saints of the living God. We (the saints) have been giving authority over all the power of our enemies. We, like Jesus, as Jesus, spoil Satan's house by casting out demons. Satan is also "not strong enough" to withstand Michael, the arch angel. Jesus, the stronger one than Satan has taken Satan strength. Satan is no longer strong enough.

Revelation 12:7-8, NIV: *⁷And there was war in heaven. Michael and his angels fought against the dragon, and the dragon and his angels fought back. ⁸But he was **not strong enough,** and they lost their place in heaven.*

In the verse above we see that "the dragon"—Satan—or his angels were "not strong enough" to withstand Michael and his angels. Why was the dragon so weak? The dragon's strength was taken away by Jesus. Jesus took the armor of his strength.

Revelation 20:1-3: *¹And I saw an angel come down from heaven, having the key of the bottomless pit and a great chain in his hand. ²And **he laid hold** on the dragon, that old serpent, which is the Devil, and Satan, and bound him a thousand years, ³and cast him into the bottomless pit, and shut him up, and set a seal upon him, that he should deceive the nations no more, till the thousand years should be fulfilled: and after that he must be loosed a little season.*

In Revelation 20:1-3, we read that the dragon, that original serpent, was "laid hold on" in order to be bound for an additional 1,000 years. The phrase "laid hold on" is also translated as "to use strength." The angel had to use strength to bind the serpent. However, we have to read the verses right. Apparently, the dragon was resisting the angel; and thus, the use of strength by the angel.

However, the strength of the angel was "stronger" and "enough" to hold the serpent in order to bind the serpent. Maybe this "angel" is Jesus the Stronger than he (Satan) that has come? Jesus, the Stronger One has "bound the strong man," according to Matthew 12:29. Satan, scorpions, serpents, demons are now subjected to us through the name of Jesus (Luke 10:17-19). That is, the Church through Jesus' name is stronger than the serpent.[31] Thus, these truths **now** exist:

---

[31] Please refer to my book, *Exousia, Your God Given Authority* for a detailed look at our God given authority

1. **"Now** is come Salvation" because Jesus took Satan's armor (his strength); and Michael the arch angel cast Satan out of heaven.

2. **"Now** is come …'power'" because Jesus took Satan's armor (his strength); and Michael the arch angel cast Satan out of heaven.

3. **"Now** is come …the kingdom of God" because Jesus took Satan's armor (his strength); and Michael the arch angel cast Satan out of heaven.

4. **"Now** is come …the 'authority' of His Christ" because Jesus took Satan's armor (his strength); and Michael the arch angel cast Satan out of heaven.

*Revelation 12:10: And I heard a loud voice saying in heaven, **Now is come salvation,** and **strength,** and the **kingdom of our God,** and the **power of his Christ**: for the accuser of our brethren is cast down, which accused them before our God day and night.*

The Prince of this World has no Place!

*John 12:31, NKJ: Now is the judgment of this world; now the **ruler of this world** will be **cast out.***

*Revelation 12:7-9, NKJ: [7]And war broke out in heaven: **Michael and his angels** fought with the dragon; and the dragon and his angels fought, [8]but they did not prevail, nor was **a place** found for them in heaven any longer. [9]**So the great dragon was cast out, that serpent of old,** called the Devil and Satan, who deceives the whole world; he was cast to the earth, and his angels were cast out with him.*

*Ephesians 4:27: Neither give **place** to the Devil.*

Jesus cast the prince of this world (the serpent) out of the world! Michael cast "that old serpent" out of heaven! Since these two statements are true, where is the place of the prince of this world? He has no legal place in the world because Jesus cast him out of the world. Satan has not place in heaven because Michael cast him. "That old serpent" also has no place with the saints; because the Bible declared in Ephesians 4:27, KJV, "Neither give place to the Devil." Therefore, the Devil has no authority over the saints of the living God.

Note: Satan has a history of "placing" himself among the sons of God. "There was a day when the sons of God came to **present (lit., place)** themselves before the LORD, and Satan came also among them to **present (lit., place) himself** before the LORD (Job 2:1). Therefore, it is not new that Satan likes to place himself among the sons of God, today. Thus, the Father's exhortation saying that we should not "give place to the Devil." This truth is also witnessed in John's vision when he was showed that a "place" was not found for the Devil and his angels in heaven anymore after Michael cast them out of heaven.

With all this truth, the Church must not allow herself to be dominated by any demonic force. We are to judge the world like Jesus judged the world by casting out devils. We are to judge angels as Jesus did by casting them out of the world into the abyss (Luke 8:28; 31; Revelation 20:3).

1 Corinthians 6:2-3: ²*Do you not know that the **saints will judge the world?** .... ³Do you not know that **we shall judge angels?** ....*

The verses above plainly declared that we would judge the world and angels. Thus, there must be a pattern; and a pattern is given by King Jesus and Michael, the arch angel. Let us look at their example; and then apply their example to our lives. We begin with Jesus' statement in John 14.

The prince of this world has **nothing (lit., "not one thing")** in Jesus! Jesus declared, "I will no longer talk much with you, for the ruler of this world is coming, and **he has nothing in Me**" (John 14:30). Jesus "was in all points tempted like as we are, yet **without sin"** **(Hebrews 4:15)**. 1 John 3:5 declares that "in Him [Jesus] is no sin." Again, the serpent has not one thing in Jesus. Thus, the serpent has no authority in or over Jesus. The serpent has been weakened by the stronger Jesus.

"For this purpose, the Son of God was manifested, that He might **destroy (lit., loose)** the works of the devil." Here is an application to believers. Colossians 2:10 declares (in the Greek text) that we "are **in Him** having been filled who is **the head** of all principalities and authorities." Those who are filled are considered as being "in" Jesus who is the Head of all principalities and authorities. It follows that if Satan has not one thing in Jesus, then Satan does not have one thing in us, through our Savior Jesus. We have authority over Satan through Jesus' headship; therefore, Satan has not place in us. Stop letting him and his demons control you!

We learned in the previous chapter that Jesus has stripped Satan of his strength and Jesus bound Satan! In Matthew 12:29, in reference to Satan, Jesus declared "how can one enter a strong man's [Satan's] house and plunder his goods, unless he first **binds** the strong man? And then he will plunder his house." Jesus **bound** Satan and plunders his house by casting out demons from the bodies of some folks. Luke 11:21-22 also declared that "when a strong man, fully armed, guards his own palace, his goods are in peace. But when a **stronger** than he comes upon him and overcomes him, **he takes from him all his armor** in which he trusted and divides his spoils."

The armor of Satan (the former strong man) was his strength to tempt. However, the **"stronger [Jesus]** than he [Satan] have come" upon Satan and took away the armor of Satan's strength. Satan is now bound in weakness; because Jesus took Satan's strength to tempt. The book of Revelation declared that Satan and his angels were "not strong enough" to stand against Michael and his angels. It appears to me that Satan was "not strong enough" to stand against Michael because Jesus already weakened Satan through overcoming Satan's temptation and through Jesus bold that was shed for us. Here is an application to believers.

Colossians 2:10 declares (in the Greek text) that we "are **in Him** having been filled **who is the head of all** principalities and authorities." Those who are "filled" are considered as being "in" Jesus who is the Head of all principalities and authorities. It follows that since our Head, Jesus, who is also the Head of all angels has showed that He is "stronger" than Satan by stripping Satan of the armor of his strength; then we "in Him" have the same authority over Satan and his angels. **Through the blood of Jesus, we are now stronger than the sin of Satan.** Jesus stripped Satan of his strength; thus, Satan pseudo strength has no place in us. Jesus "did rescue us **out of the authority of the darkness and** did **translate us** into the reign of the Son of His love." (Colossians 1:13, YLT).

Jesus cast Satan out of this world; and the saints are to do the same to Satan! [30]"Jesus answered and said, "This voice did not come because of Me, but for your sake. [31]"**Now** is the judgment of this world; **now** the ruler of this world will be **cast out**" (John 12:30-31). Satan has no place in the world either. He has been cast out of the world. Paul declared in 1 Corinthians 6:2 that the saints shall judge the world. The logical question is what is Jesus' pattern of judging the world?

Jesus judged the world by casting out the ruler of the world. Thus, the saints are to judge the world by casting out principalities, authorities, powers, controllers, world-rulers, spiritual 'hurts' in heavenly places, and so on. In effect, casting demons out of the world is also the same as judging angels. We are admonished not to give place to the Devil. The same is true for Satan's angels. We are not to give them place. Michael, the arch angel did not give Satan or his angel any place in heaven.

Michael, the arch angel cast Satan out of heaven, because Satan is "not strong enough" to tangle with Michael! [7]"And there was war in heaven. Michael and his angels fought against the dragon, and the dragon and his angels fought back. [8]But he was not **strong enough,** and they lost their place in heaven. [9]The great dragon was hurled down—that ancient serpent called the devil, or Satan, who leads the whole world astray. He was hurled to the earth, and his angels with him." (Revelation 12:7-9, NIV).

We learned earlier that Jesus, the "stronger than he (Satan)," stripped Satan of his amour (his strength) (Luke 11:19-22). Since Jesus stripped Satan of the armor of his strength, Satan is "not strong enough" any longer. Thus, Michael was able to defeat Satan because the Devils is "not strong enough" to prevail. This was not the first encounter between the Devil and Michael.

After Moses death, the Devil attempted to seize the body of Moses. However, Michael intervened and rebuked Satan through the Lord's authority (Jude 1:9). The same is true for all believers today. The Devil has no authority over your body. He also has no place in your heavenly places afforded you in Christ. We now "sit together in **heavenly places** in Christ Jesus" (Ephesians 2:6). Yet, our warfare is "against principalities," "against 'authorities,'" "against 'world-strengths' of the darkness of this age" and "against spiritual hosts of wickedness **in the heavenly places**" (Ephesians 6:12). Thus, Michael and his angels also aid us in the heavenly places, like he did for Daniel.

Daniel, the beloved prophet, also encountered some heavenly disturbances from the principality of Persia; and Michael had to come and "bind" the prince of Persia who was attempting to stop another arch angel, Gabriel from imparting to Daniel "what is noted in the Scripture of Truth." The book of Revelation declared that Michael and his angel eventually cast Satan and his angel out of heaven. The results of Michael casting out Satan from heaven were impressive. Salvation came! Power came! The kingdom of God came! The authority of His Christ came! Jesus' blood is magnified! Hear the Scriptures of Revelation 12:7-11, NIV!

> *7And there was war in heaven. Michael and his angels fought against the dragon, and the dragon and his angels fought back. 8But **he was not strong enough,** and they **lost their place in heaven.** 9The great dragon was hurled down – that ancient serpent called the devil, or Satan, who leads the whole world astray. He was hurled to the earth, and his angels with him. 10Then I heard a loud voice in heaven say: "**Now have come the salvation** and **the power** and **the kingdom of our God,** and **the authority of his Christ.** For the accuser of our brothers, who accuses them before our God day and night, has been hurled down. 11They **overcame him by the blood of the Lamb** and by the word of their testimony; they did not love their lives so much as to shrink from death* **(Revelation 12:7-11, NIV).**

Here is an application to believers. Jesus declared that whenever His disciples cast out devils from people, Satan falls from heaven simultaneously. Thus, the authority to cast out demons is linked to Satan falling from heaven.

Luke 10:17-19, NIV: *17The seventy-two returned with joy and said,* **"Lord, even the demons submit to us in your name."** *18He replied, "I* **saw Satan fall like lightning from heaven.** *19I* **have given you authority** *to trample on snakes and scorpions and to overcome all the power of the enemy; nothing will harm you.*

When the seventy returned declaring how demons submit to them through Jesus' name, Jesus replied by saying that He saw Satan "**fall**" like lightning from heaven. "Fall" is written in the imperfect tense in the Greek texts. Thus, the verse can read as such: "I saw Satan **'falling'** from heaven." That is Satan's "falling" is continuous. Saying it another way, as the Seventy were casting out the demons, there was a simultaneous action in the heavens; Satan is falling from the heaven. Yes, when we cast out demons from people in the earth, simultaneously, Satan is falling from heaven.

We have authority to also displace demons from the heavenly places, by the authority Jesus have given us through His Word and His blood.

The blood of Jesus overcomes Satan! "⁹So the great dragon was cast out, that serpent of old, called the Devil and Satan, who deceives the whole world; he was cast to the earth, and his angels were cast out with him. ¹⁰Then I heard a loud voice saying in heaven, now salvation, and strength, and the kingdom of our God, and the power of His Christ have come, for the accuser of our brethren, who accused them before our God day and night, has been cast down. ¹¹**And they overcame him by the blood of the Lamb** and by the word of their testimony, and they did not love their lives to the death" **(Revelation 12:9-11).**

As the Philistines in 1 Samuel 17 could not pass the place called "Ephes Dammin" ("boundary of bloods"), so Satan is overcome by the blood of the Lamb. Satan cannot pass the boundary of the blood of Jesus. The book of Hebrews 12:24 declare that the blood of Jesus "speaks 'stronger' things." Yes, Jesus' blood is "better" and "stronger" than any strengths of the enemy. Through His cross, Jesus "disarmed the powers and authorities, he made a public spectacle of them, triumphing over them by the cross" **(Colossians 2:15, NIV).**

Thus, Jesus marginalized Satan; and the Church is to do the same. We should focus on the triumph of Jesus, and the authority of Jesus. In this age, ministers preach more about Satan than they do the all-powerful God. All of God's ministers need to preach a **mega God** and less and less about Satan pseudo controls. Preachers need to declare the strength of Jesus. If they are going to mention the Devil, declare how weak he is to Jesus and Jesus' blood. Jesus declared in Matthew 28:18: "**All authority** has been given to Me in heaven and on earth."

We are to declare the message of Jesus knowing that Satan has no place in the world or in heaven; knowing that Jesus holds all authority, now. The Bible contains about three-quarters of a million words. Satan and his associated names are mentioned significantly **less than** 0.1% of the time. If God marginalizes the tempter in His Word, so should the Church. Jesus is the head of all principalities and powers and He "triumphed" over them on the cross.

That is, Jesus stripped, disarmed, displaced Satan and all his angels; and Jesus paraded them naked in chains and made a public spectacle of them. Satan no longer has any place or authority in us, in the world or in heaven. The house of Jesus is waxing stronger and stronger (2 Samuel 3:1), and Satan and his angels are waxing weaker and weaker! With that said, here are some examples that demonstrate that Satan has no place among us.

In 2011 a young man came to me requesting prayer. He relayed to me how he was losing his mind and how something was taking over his body. He was so demonically influenced that he was jailed for losing his mind and going out into the street naked. After I listened to his story, I laid my hand on him and prayed for him by casting out the demon in the name of Jesus Christ. He became stiff as a board and fell to the sofa as the spirit left him. After he came to himself, he said that he was shivering and felt very cold (I gave him a shirt to warm himself); he also could not look at the light of the day for a few moment (apparently the spirit that was oppressing him had cover his spiritual eyes and natural eyes with literal darkness).

Recently, my wife (Judith) had an encounter with a lady at a women's meeting. This lady happened to be standing beside my wife and the Lord asked my wife to show the lady love. Soon after my wife had showed the lady love, by hugging her and praying for the lady, the lady began to convulse, contort, and speak in a strange demonic tongue, as the demons (including a python spirit) in this lady manifested. My wife commanded the demons to go back to the abyss! My wife eventually asked the demons that were manifesting, "Why did you come? Why did you come here?" To which the demons in the woman refused to respond by locking up the woman's body; however, the demon answered the question by the action demonstrated by the woman. The woman began to thrust her pelvic area as if having sexual intercourse. At which point, my wife began to cast out the demons in Jesus' name. Judith told one demon after another to come out in the name of Jesus. In response, the demons attempted to physically take the woman's body with them as they were leaving. The woman started screaming, coughing, throwing up, her head going back and forth in a violent motion, her eyes rolling in the back of her head, legs kicking as each unclean spirit left her. The demons were completely subjected and bound to the name of Jesus. In the encounter with this the woman Judith asked the lady to repent and to accept Jesus as her Savoir.

As indicated in this chapter, Satan and his angels have no place. They have no place in the world because Jesus cast them out of the world. They have not place in heaven, Michael and his angels cast out Satan and his angels. Satan and his angels have no place in the Church. The Holy Spirit by Paul commanded us not to "give place to the Devil." Satan and his angels have to obey the Church when they cast them out of people in the name of Jesus. Satan and his angels cannot renter a person if we command them not to enter no more. Therefore, through the authority of Jesus, we cast out angels, authorities, powers, wicked spirits, etc. from those who are demonized, and these devils have no place in people, in the world, or in heaven.

Mark 9:25-27: [25]*When Jesus saw that the people came running together, He rebuked the unclean spirit, saying to it, "Deaf and dumb spirit, I command you, come out of him and **enter him no more!**"[26]Then the spirit **cried out, convulsed** him greatly, and **came out of him**. And he became as one dead, so that many said, "He is dead." [27]But Jesus took him by the hand and lifted him up, and he arose.*

Do not Bring Railing Accusation

Jude 1:8-10: *[8]Likewise also these filthy dreamers defile the flesh, despise* **dominion,** *and speak evil of* **dignities.** *[9]Yet Michael the archangel, when contending with the Devil he disputed about the body of Moses,* **does not bring against him** **a railing accusation,** *but said, the Lord rebuke you. [10]But these speak evil of those things which they know not: but what they know naturally, as brute beasts, in those things they corrupt themselves.*

Believe it or not, the Devil is also considered a "dominion" and "dignitary." It is prudent therefore to follow the examples in the Bible as to how we rebuke the Devil. We are not to bring against him a railing accusation. "Railing accusation" literally means "blasphemy" or "evil speaking."

Thus, as Michael the archangel exemplified, we are not to "blaspheme" ("bring … a railing accusation") even against the Devil. Michael left all evil speaking towards the Devil to the Lord's authority. "The Lord rebukes you (Satan)" will suffice. Or, like our Lord Jesus you may say to Satan "get you 'under'" **(Matthew 4:10);** or you may say like the Lord Jesus, "Get behind me Satan" **(Matthew 16:23).**

In Zechariah 3, the same example is followed by the "angel of the Lord." The angel of the Lord invoked the name of the Lord to rebuke Satan. And, Satan had to stand down, he could proceed no further to resist or accuse Joshua.

Zechariah3:1-2, NIV: *Then he showed me Joshua the high priest standing before the angel of the LORD, and Satan standing at his right side to accuse him. [2]***The LORD said** *to Satan,* **"The LORD rebuke** *you, Satan!* **The LORD,** *who has chosen Jerusalem,* **rebuke you!** *Is not this man a burning stick snatched from the fire?"*

Growing up in the Church in the 1980s, it was common to hear preachers rail against Satan, a habit we all learned. However, even though Satan is our enemy, and he is dangerous;[32] there are still certain ways in the kingdom of God by which the Lord Himself,

---

[32] See Revelation 2:10; Revelation 12:17-13:2; Revelation 16:13-14.

archangels, and the angel of the Lord rebuked Satan; a point which the writer of Jude is attempting to convey.

Again, this does not mean that we do not resist the Devil. Satan is indeed dangerous and a killer (Revelation 2:10; Revelation 12:2-4; Revelation 12:17-13:4; 1 Thessalonians 2:18; 1 Peter 5:8, etc.). The Bible is clear, stating that once we submit to God, we have the authority to **"resist** the Devil." "Submit yourselves therefore to God. **Resist the Devil**, and he will flee from you" **(James 4:7).**

Michael rebuked the Devil through the Lord Jesus; and the Devil apparently fled[33] and left the body of Moses with Michael. How do I know that Moses body was left with Michael? The Lord Himself buried Moses (Deuteronomy 34: 5-6). Moses and Elijah also appeared "in glory" to/with Jesus on the mountain; thus, the Lord must have resurrected Moses after the Devil tried to steal Moses's body (Luke 9; Matthew 17). James 4:7 says that we are to resist the Devil and he will flee. Thus, when Michael rebuked the Devil by the Lord Jesus, the Devil was put in his place—"behind" Jesus and "under" Jesus (Matthew 4).

We must do the same. We must rebuke Satan and all his angels in the name of the Lord Jesus Christ. Except let us follow the "non-blasphemous" pattern of our Lord and the elect angels. Do not blaspheme dominions and glories. The Lord Jesus will judge Satan in the Lord's time (Matthew 25:41, Revelation 20:3; 10).

Luke 10:17-24: [17]*And the seventy returned again with joy, saying, Lord, even the* **devils are subject unto us through thy name.** [18]*And he said unto them,* **I beheld Satan as lightning fall from heaven.** [19]*Behold, I give unto you power to tread on* **serpents** *and scorpions, and over all the power of the enemy: and nothing shall by any means hurt you.* [20]**Notwithstanding in this rejoice not, that the spirits are subject unto you; but rather rejoice, because your names are written in heaven.** [21]*In that hour Jesus rejoiced in spirit, and said, I thank you O Father, Lord of heaven and earth, that you have hid these things from the wise and prudent, and have revealed them unto babes: even so, Father; for so it seemed good in thy sight.* [22]*All things are delivered to me of my*

---

[33] See James 4:7

Father: and no man knows who the Son is, but the Father; and who the Father is, but the Son, and he to whom the Son will reveal him. 23And he turned him unto his disciples, and said privately, blessed are the eyes which see the things that you see: 24For I tell you, that many prophets and kings have desired to see those things which you see, and have not seen them; and to hear those things which you hear, and have not heard them.

God Controls the Serpent

There are a lot of believers who thinks that Satan is on the same level as God. How can a created being be equal to its Creator? Satan has no power except what is allowed by God; and yes, sometimes the serpent oversteps his boundary. Yet in all this, the serpent is subjected to God, the Father. God controls all His creation. Leviathan with its "heads" represents Satan with his "seven heads" is "a servant" to God, the Father "forever."

*Psalm 74:14: You break the **heads** of **leviathan** in pieces and gave him to be meat to the people inhabiting the wilderness.*

*Job 41:1-5: ¹Canst you draw out leviathan with a hook? Or his tongue with a cord which you let down? ²Canst you put a hook into his nose? Or bore his jaw through with a thorn? ³Will he make many supplications unto thee? Will he speak soft words unto thee? ⁴Will he make a covenant with thee? Will you take him **for a servant** forever? ⁵Wilt you play with him as with a bird? Or will you bind him for thy maidens?*

Again, in the verse above see that Leviathan, the serpent is a **"servant forever"** to God. In Job 1:12 and Job 2:6, we also learn that it was **God** who gave Satan permission to test Job. Satan had to get permission from Jesus to "sift" Peter (see Luke 22:31-32). Satan could not touch Job or Peter without, Jesus' permission or the Father's permission in the entire situation.

I reiterate that Satan had to ask for permission from God to touch Job and Peter. In Matthew 4, concerning the temptation of Jesus, it was the **Holy Spirit** that "led" Jesus to be tempted of the Devil. The tempter was limited in his access to Jesus. In fact, as we learned previously, Satan and his angels were bound by Jesus; and Jesus spoiled Satan's house by casting out demons (see Mark 3:26-27).

The serpent and his angels are also totally subjected to the name of Jesus (1 Peter 3:22). The saints now hold control over Satan through Jesus. In Luke 10:17-20, we learn that the demons and Satan are subject to Jesus' disciple through the name of Jesus. The apostle Paul exercised use and control over Satan. Paul had apostolic authority to "deliver" the unrepentant over to Satan for the literal destruction of the flesh (1 Corinthians 5:5). Paul also demonstrated authority to deliver "blasphemers" to Satan for discipline, or training (I Timothy 1:20). This truth also shows, as previously stated, that the serpent is indeed created to be serve humanity from the beginning.

1 Corinthians 5:1-5: ¹It is reported commonly that there is fornication among you, and such fornication as is not so much as named among the Gentiles, that one should have his father's wife. ²And you are puffed up, and have not rather mourned, that he that hath done this deed might be taken away from among you. ³For I verily, as absent in body, but present in spirit, have judged already, as though I were present, concerning him that hath so done this deed, ⁴in the name of our Lord Jesus Christ, when you are gathered together, and my spirit, with the power of our Lord Jesus Christ, ⁵to deliver such a one unto Satan for the destruction of the flesh, that the spirit may be saved in the day of the Lord Jesus.

1 Timothy 1:18-20: ¹⁸This charge I commit unto thee, son Timothy, according to the prophecies which went before on thee, that you by them might war a good warfare; ¹⁹holding faith, and a good conscience; which some having put away concerning faith have made shipwreck: ²⁰Of whom is Hymenaeus and Alexander; whom I have delivered unto Satan, that they may learn not to blaspheme.

Contrary to popular belief, Satan is not in control of us. God, the Father, the Holy Spirit, and Jesus have absolute control over the tempter. Apostles (of the Lamb or of the Spirit) were also grated authority to use Satan for discipline, according to the "authority God has given them" (2 Corinthians 13:10). Jesus' believers and the elect angels all have authority, through Jesus, to exercise control over Satan and all spirit enemies according to Luke 10:17-20. Jesus is the Lord (lit., controller) of all.

The Boundary of Jesus' Blood

1 Samuel 17:1-3: *¹Now the **Philistines** gathered together their armies to battle, and were gathered together at Shochoh, which belongs to Judah, and pitched between Shochoh and Azekah, in **Ephesdammim.** ²And Saul and the men of Israel were gathered together, and pitched by the valley of Elah, and set the battle in array against the Philistines. ³And the Philistines stood on a mountain on the one side, and Israel stood on a mountain on the other side: and there was a valley between them.*

Jesus' blood that He shed for us is a boundary that Satan cannot cross or defeat. In the days of David and Saul, the Philistines (enemies of the Israelites) gathered against them. The Philistines could only pitch their tents in a place called "Ephes Dammim" — "boundary of bloods." These enemies of Israel could not pass the boundary of the blood. The same is true for the "Israel of God" — His Church. Satan cannot go pass the boundary of the blood of Jesus.

Revelation 12:9; 11: *And the great dragon was cast out, that old serpent, called the Devil, and Satan, which deceives the whole world: he was cast out into the earth, and his angels were cast out with him …. And **they overcame him by the blood of the Lamb,** and by the word of their testimony; and they loved not their lives unto the death.*

The blood of Jesus conquers! The saints "overcame" (lit., "conquered") Satan by the blood of the Lamb! The great dragon cannot, and I repeat, cannot cross the boundary set by the blood of Jesus! We conquer through the blood of Jesus. Jesus' blood washed us from our sins; thus, His blood is now a boundary against sin (Revelation 1:5). In any battle, the blood of Jesus serves as a boundary that Satan and his angels cannot cross as it was in the days of David and as it was from the beginning. From the beginning, Jesus made the Devil defeated with respect to His better-governing blood of Jesus. That is, the blood of Jesus is stronger than the serpent from before the serpent's beginning. Allow me to show an explain.

According to Genesis 2:19 and Genesis 3:1, we learned the beasts of the field were made from the "ground;" and that the serpent which was a part of these "beasts of the field." "And out of the **ground** the LORD God formed every beast of the field ...." "Now the serpent was **more** subtle **than** any beast of the field which the LORD God had made."

As we learned in an earlier chapter, one of the significant phrases in Genesis 3:1 is the phrase **"more ... than."** These two words were translated from **one** Hebrew word—**min or minniy or minney** (Strong's # 4480, NIV Exhaustive Concordance #4946). The word literally means "a **part of**; hence (prep) from or **out of.**"

Thus, the verse could read, "The serpent was crafty **'out of'** all (the) beast of the field...." Or "the serpent was crafty **'a part of'** all (the) beast of the field ...." Therefore, the serpent was one of the beasts that were made from the **"ground."**

"Ground" is the Hebrew word ADaMaH (המדא). Hebrew letters are made up of pictures. We call it hieroglyphics. The hieroglyphic picture for the word "ground" is a picture of "what comes from" (ה) "strong" (א) "blood" (מד). This "strong blood" is the "stronger ... blood" of Jesus. The book of Hebrews teaches that "you are come ... to Jesus the mediator of the new covenant, and to the **blood of sprinkling, which speaks better (lit., "stronger") things** than that of Abel" (Hebrews 12:22-24).

The "ground" was somehow related to blood, even as "water" is also associated with blood; and this blood is the stronger blood of Jesus. Therefore, these beasts that came from the "ground" are weak to the stronger blood of Jesus. Meaning, they were created weaker to the governmental blood of Jesus. Jesus' blood has always been a boundary that Satan or spirit enemies cannot cross.

The boundary of Jesus' blood is so powerful that an entire army cannot cross it. This is exemplified by the philistine's army in the days of David and Saul when the Philistine army could not cross the boundary of the bloods. The Philistines could only pitch their tents in a place called "Ephes Dammim"—"boundary of bloods."

With that said, here is a personal experience of the boundary of Jesus' blood that cannot be crossed.

During the early 1990s, we were in Pennsylvania visiting friends and ministering. We were in a home and the lady of the house was concerned that someone she knew was using what the Bile calls "curious arts" or "magic" against her **(compare Acts 8; Acts 13, Acts 19).** She asked me to pray, so we prayed and declared that anyone that means her harm cannot come through her doors. That day, a man she knew visited her home (the lady believed that this man was one of the persons using curious arts against her).

As the man attempted to enter her home, he was knocked backward repeatedly. He would try repeatedly to enter the house, and the hand of God or an angel knocked him backward again and again several times. Eventually, the man became frustrated and left because no matter how many times he attempted to enter the home, he could not. As we saw this man being prevented by the invisible hand of God to enter the home (apparently, he meant her and us harm), we all stood in awe at the work of the Holy Spirit who is eternally linked to the blood of Jesus **(Hebrews 9:14).** This is proof that demons and those satanically motivated are restricted by the boundary set by the blood of Jesus.

The disciples of Jesus Christ are authorized to utilize "Ephes Dammim" — the "boundary of the bloods" (plural) that was shed by Jesus. Yes, Jesus shed His blood for us more than once.

1. He shed His blood in the garden. "And being in an agony he prayed more earnestly: and His sweat was as it were great drops of **blood** falling down to the ground" (Luke 22:44).

2. He shed His blood after being speared. "But one of the soldiers with a spear pierced His side, and forthwith came there out **blood** and water" (John 19:34).

3. He shed His blood being nailed to the cross. "And, having made peace through the **blood** of His cross ..." (**Colossians 1:20 w/John 20:25-27; Luke 24:39).** "This man was handed

over to you by God's set purpose and foreknowledge; and you, with the help of wicked men, put him to death by **nailing** him to the cross" **(Acts 2:23, NIV)**.

Jesus' blood-sweat that was shed during His prayer in the garden is a boundary for us. Jesus' blood that was shed when He was speared on the cross is a boundary for us. Jesus' blood that was shed on the cross through the nails in His hands and His feet is a boundary for us. **We overcome … by the blood of the Lamb! The blood of Jesus is stronger! The blood of Jesus is a boundary to us that no evil thing can cross! Jesus is Lord of all!**

Other Books

Wisdom from Above, by Judith Peart
Procreation, Understanding Sex, and Identity, by Judith Peart
100 Nevers, by Judith Peart
The Shattered and the Healing by Judith Peart
The Lamb, by Donald Peart
Jesus' Resurrection, Our Inheritance, by Donald Peart.
Sexuality, By Donald Peart
Forgiven 490 Times, by Donald Peart w/Judith Peart!
The Days of the Seventh Angel, By Donald Peart
The Torah (The Principle) of Giving, by Donald Peart
The Time Came, by Donald Peart
The Last Hour, the First Hour, the Forty-Second Generation, by Donald Peart
Vision Real, by Donald Peart
The False Prophet, Alias, Another Beast V1, by Donald Peart
"the beast," by Donald Peart
Son of Man Prophesy Against the false prophet, by Donald Peart
The Red Dragon's Tail—The Prophets who Teach Lies, by Donald Peart
The Work of Lawlessness Revealed, by Donald Peart
When the Lord Made the Tempter, by Donald Peart
Examining Doctrine, Volume 1, by Donald Peart
Exousia, Your God Given Authority, by Donald Peart
The Numbers of God, by Donald Peart
The Completions of the Ages … by Donald Peart
The Revelation of Jesus Christ, by Donald Peart
Jude—Translation and Commentary, by Donald Peart
Obtaining the Better Resurrection, by Donald Peart
Manifestations from Our Lord Jesus ...by Donald and Judith Peart).
Obtaining the Better Resurrection, by Donald Peart
The New Testament, Dr. Donald Peart Exegesis
The Tree of Life, By Dr. Donald Peart
The Spirit and Power of John, the Baptist by Dr. Donald Peart
The Shattered and the Healing by Judith Peart
Is She Married to a Husband? by Donald Peart
The Ugliest Man God Made by Donald Peart
Does Answering the Call of God Impact Your Children? by Donald Peart
Victory Out-of-the Beast-the Harvest of the Earth by Donald Peart
The Order of Melchizedek by Donald Peart
Ezekiel-the House-the City-the Land (Interpreting the Patterns), by Donald Peart
Butter and Honey, Understanding how to Choose the Good and Refuse Evil

Contact Information:

Crown of Glory Ministries
P.O. Box 1041 Randallstown, MD 21133
donaldpeart7@gmail.com

About the Author

Donald Peart is married to Judith Peart. Donald committed his life (though for a short period) while Judith recommitted her life to the Lord Jesus around the summer of 1981 after the pair kept reading the book of John and the book of Revelation. Donald read the entire book of Revelation and became especially interested in Revelation 20:4. Eventually, in April 1986, Donald and Judith permanently recommitted their lives to the Lord Jesus. They have been serving the Lord Jesus since and declaring the well-message of Jesus, the Christ. Over the years, the Lord Jesus has worked various manifestations of signs, wonders, and miracles through them. Below are three examples of the Lord Jesus' involvement in the lives of Donald and Judith.

In 1988, while living in North Carolina, the voice of the Lord spoke to Donald and said, "I have not called you to be an apostle, pastor, evangelist, teacher, but a …(Donald blocked out the rest of the words the Lord was speaking to Him; because at the time, Donald was afraid God would call him to function in a ministry contrary to what Donald believed he should be functioning as--a prophet)." Approximately seventeen years later, on February 6, 2005, in Maryland, while Donald was on a fast; on the 13th day of the fast, the Lord Jesus resumed the conversation he had with Donald in 1988. As Donald listened, the voice of the Lord continued exactly as He spoke in 1988, "I have not called you to be a prophet, an apostle, an evangelist, a pastor, or teacher, but I have called you to be a son."

In 1990, while in prayer speaking to the heavenly Father about going to university to study engineering, Donald heard the Lord Jesus say to him "you are as Joseph before me; go to engineering school; you will be good at it." The Lord also said to Donald, "this is the sign that I have spoken to you; your wife is pregnant with a girl." Donald responded to the Lord saying, "Joseph did not have any daughters." To which the Lord replied, "Joseph is a fruitful son, a fruitful son by a well whose daughters run over the wall." Donald immediately searched the Scriptures to see if Joseph had any daughters. The Scriptures confirmed that what the Lord spoke to Donald was correct. Genesis 49:22, translated from the Hebrew, states "Joseph is a fruitful son, a fruitful son by a well whose daughters run over the wall." The "sign" the Lord gave to Donald was fulfilled immediately. Judith Peart was already pregnant with their third child; a girl named Charity was born to them according to the time of life. Donald also graduated from engineering school. In addition to their five natural children, they have spiritual "daughters" and "sons " because God is fulfilling

His word to them. This was also the second and third time the Lord called Donald a son.

On a day around 1991, Donald became disheartened, and he spoke to the Lord about his circumstances. At the time, he and his wife were experiencing extreme trials after Donald's obedience to the Lord. Donald was instructed to study God's Word exclusively, which turned out to be almost four years of intense study and prayer coupled with a time of consistent acute trials or probe-testing. As Donald sat on the sofa that day reading Genesis 2, the Lord began unveiling to Donald an understanding of Genesis 2 with an understanding he had not heard the elders teach. The Spirit of the Lord began to show Donald the sequence of creation, including the man (Adam), the original serpent, and Mrs. Adam (later called Eve). As the Spirit of Jesus revealed to Donald how the Scriptures in Genesis 2 should be interpreted, his mind began questioning what he was reading and hearing in the Spirit. His mind questioned the revelation of the Holy Spirit due to previous doctrines he learned in church from the elders and commentaries. As Donald questioned the understanding the Spirit of God revealed to him, Donald saw the pages of the Bible he was reading being closed one by one, yet the physical Bible in his lap was still opened to the same pages he was reading. This is when he realized he was seeing a vision. The Lord then said to him, "Do not filter My Word through what the elders have taught you."

As a result of the Lord making Himself know to Donald and Judith throughout the years and providing explicit directions to Donald with regards God's doctrine, Donald and Judith have preached the gospel of Christ as the Lord has taught him; a gospel that is centered on Jesus Christ, the Son of the living God and the bride of Christ. With that said, the Lord Jesus has also graced Donald Peart to earn diplomas from Baltimore Polytechnic High School; an Associate of Arts degree in Pre-Engineering, a Bachelor of Science degree in Civil Engineering, a Master of Divinity, a Master of Science in Construction Management, and a Doctorate in Theology.